PERSONAL
SURVIVAL

TEACHINGS OF
THE ORDER OF CHRISTIAN MYSTICS

PERSONAL SURVIVAL

TEACHINGS OF THE ORDER OF CHRISTIAN MYSTICS

THE "CURTISS BOOKS" FREELY AVAILABLE AT

WWW.ORDEROFCHRISTIANMYSTICS.CO.ZA

At the request of students, this latest photograph of Dr. F. Homer Curtiss
is thus published for all.

PERSONAL SURVIVAL

WITH PHYSICAL PROOFS

BY
F. HOMER CURTISS, B.S., M.D.
Founder of
THE UNIVERSAL RELIGIOUS FELLOWSHIP, INC.

2014 EDITION

REPUBLISHED FOR THE ORDER BY
MOUNT LINDEN PUBLISHING
JOHANNESBURG, SOUTH AFRICA
ISBN: 978-1-920483-18-0

"Ministers of Christ and Stewards of the Mysteries of God."
1 Corinthians 4 vs. 1

TABLE OF CONTENTS

PREFACE

In response to the thousands of letters of inquiry, curiosity, fear, rebellion and despair received by the authors since the publication of the many editions of our *Realms of the Living Dead*, we herewith present further details, with many physical proofs as to personal survival after so-called death. This is done in order to answer the inquiries, quell the rebellion, dispel the fears and bring comfort through understanding, to those who have lost loved ones, either in war, accident, suicide or disease, or in the inevitable withdrawal from the physical realm which ends advanced age.

CONFLICTING REPORTS:

Because of the many conflicting reports given by mediums as to conditions in the invisible worlds of the after-life, there is much confusion about such reports in the public mind. Therefore, in *Realms of the Living Dead* we endeavored to clarify this confusion by organizing the discovered facts by a regular series of investigations. This revealed the fact that there are as many, and even more, different and distinct regions in the invisible worlds as there are in a great city, such as the retail district, wholesale district, factory district, athletic fields and the slums.

A visitor exploring one of these districts might correctly claim that his description of that particular district revealed the character of the city; whereas it would reveal only that limited section which he had visited. In a similar way reports of isolated mediums reveal only the tiny section of the after life and its conditions which they were enabled to contact by their degree of development.

THE SEVEN REALMS:

To simplify our investigation, in *Realms of the Living Dead*, we divided the after-world, commonly called the astral world, into seven regions, which we call *realms*, and give a description of the characteristics of each of these realms, together with the approximate number of miles each realm extends above the earth's surface.[1] Although these regions overlap as do the regions of the city, nevertheless their general conditions are just as characteristic as are those of the city. Thus we find that all the mediums' reports may be true as far as they go but represent only limited regions, – not the whole.

It should be remembered that the world entered through the gate of death includes as many states of consciousness, and even more, than the physical world, which is entered through the gate of birth; for birth into the Physical World is death to the Astral World, just as death to the Physical World is birth to the Astral World.

INVESTIGATORS LIMITED:

As we have explained in the *Realms of the Living Dead*, while many of the teachings herein given find confirmation in the several works on psychic phenomena and after-death conditions recently published, many of the scientists who have investigated this subject have not yet discovered all the facts herein explained, because they have no all-inclusive *Cosmic Soul Science* to guide them, and because they are content to wander aimlessly, without any guiding light, in the lower regions of the Astral World where the great spiritual teachers are seldom, if ever, found. Their investigations, sincere and honest as they may be, are much like laboriously searching through the plebeian section of a great city for a scientist or professor who could explain the conditions met with, when all that would be necessary would be to take a taxi through the slums, to the University, where hundreds of professors who are authorities on all types of knowledge

---

[1] See *Realms of the Living Dead*, Curtiss, 181.

are to be found. Indeed, few psychic investigators ask their way to such centers of learning, or even realize that such exist in the Higher Worlds.

In this volume we do not present additional details, but give actual physical proofs that our teachings about personal survival are not merely theory and speculation or mediums' "say-so" but are facts scientifically investigated and *physically proved*.

The physical proofs we shall present herein do not depend on the reports of the psychics, however evidential they may seem, or upon the opinions, education, or mentality of the medium. These proofs, therefore, eliminate the claim that such reports may have emanated from the medium's sub-conscious or superconscious mind, or from the mind of some other living person, by telepathy, instead of from some entirely different and discarnate personality.

As one noted writer says, "The aim of any worthwhile teaching is the acquisition, not of *psychic powers*, but of a manner of living. What the people need is a presentation of the truth, in the light of their own times, and terms of their knowledge; so that each may seek truth's comfort for himself, and find it."[2]

And so with this thought in mind we present the following chapters on Personal Survival.

---

[2] *Across the Unknown*, White, 280.

CHAPTER I

COSMIC PHILOSOPHY

Great are the symbols of being, but that which is
symboled is greater;
Vast the create and beheld, but vaster the inward
creator;
Back of the sound broods the silence, back of the gift
stands the giving;
Back of the hand that receives thrill the sensitive
nerves of receiving.

Space is as nothing to spirit, the deed is outdone by
the doing;
The heart of the wooer is warm, but warmer the heart
of the wooing;
And up from the pits where these shiver, and up from
the heights where those shine
Twin voices and shadow swim starward, and the
essence of life is divine.

Indirection, RICHARD REALF

For the benefit of those who have not been students
of the Cosmic Soul Science of our *Universal Religious
Fellowship*, we will give a brief summary of the philosophy which underlies all manifestation, as a background to
our specific subject.

The object of philosophy is to determine a reasonable connection between cause and effect;
therefore philosophy is concerned with finding out the
origin, reason, meaning and purpose of the Universe.

The mere recital of the many kinds of spirit phenomena, no matter how scientifically presented and physically proved, is not sufficient to give a comprehensive view of the meaning and significance of personal survival, and the origin and causation of such phenomena. Hence at least an outline of the philosophy, which underlies these manifestations, is necessary.

Cosmic Concept:

We must establish certain basic principles by means of which we can organize the multitudinous and complex manifestations into an organic whole, and thus give us a comprehensive view of all manifestation, both here and hereafter. Only thus can our consciousness expand to give us the Cosmic Concept of life as a whole. We will thus be able to push back the frontiers of our knowledge and grasp ever greater realization of Reality and Truth. This will enable us to ascend even higher up the Mount of Attainment, where we can obtain ever wider bird's eye views of the whole scheme of creation, in truly comprehensive divine realization. Without such a Cosmic Concept we will be endlessly focussing our time and attention on one detail after another, and thus will not be able to see the forest, because we are too close to the trees.

To the mass of thinking people who are seeking some satisfying answer to the problems of life, there comes from out of the ages the Teachings of those Great Souls who reached their Godlike state before this world was born. These Great Souls have always been and still are, the Guides and Teachers of mankind, hence those whose reason postulates, or whose intuition recognizes such Godlike Beings, can safely accept their Teachings, for they are in a position to know the Truth.

It is these Teachings which form the basis of the Author's Cosmic Soul Science expounded within.

"Man has a spiritual evolution which comes from above,

and a material evolution, which belongs to this earth. His physical body is the highest attainment of a physical evolution through all the lower kingdoms. . . . His spiritual evolution is the result of voluntary descent of Immortal Egos into more or less perfected bodies,—human—animal bodies—, and their subsequent efforts to control and spiritualize these animal organisms." [1] A little careful consideration will reveal this.

LIFE IMMORTAL:

There is no life force, consciousness, creative power or ability to originate in matter itself. Forms appear out of the unseen, seemingly self-generated, manifest for a limited cycle to accomplish their purpose, then disintegrate and disappear, leaving behind only the ash or the mineral elements out of which they were formed. But *no life dies*; only the form through which a particular aspect of life temporarily manifested, "dies," for life is immortal and can never die. The form dies not because of lack of life, but because of more life than it can express. For one reason or another that form is no longer a suitable vehicle for its aspect of life force, and upon the withdrawal of that integrating and cohesive power, the form disintegrates. For this reason *all forms of physical phenomena are impermanent and transitory*; in a state of constant flux and change, a constant becoming.

That which we see in the physical world is therefore but the outer husk or shell, the vehicle, or mechanism by and through which some unseen cause, some ideal or pattern, some center of life, consciousness and force from the unseen worlds, is striving to manifest for a time in the seen.

Just as the idea or mental pattern of a building is created in the mental world, by the mind of the architect, and as the automobile or other invention, painting, statue, or sonata first exists in the mind of the creator, so does the pattern of

---

[1] *Voice of Isis*, Curtiss, 229.

every manifested thing exist in the unseen worlds before it descends through the various realms of manifestation on Earth.

This goes to show that all manifestation is an expression of various types of personalized intelligence, which is eternally seeking the expression of ideals in all realms, from the fashioners of the minute details, up to that Infinite Consciousness, which has planned, and directs and supports the manifestation of all that we speak of under the all inclusive term *God*.

Preexistence:

It is therefore, a basic principle of the philosophy of our Cosmic Soul Science, that all manifested things appear on Earth out of the unseen, according to the law of Materialization. This is accomplished through the law of Unfoldment called growth. It is obvious therefore, that the Earth Plane is not the Plane of Origin or Causation. It is only the Plane of physical manifestation of that which existed beforehand in the higher, finer, invisible, spiritual and mental worlds of Origin or Causation.

As one philosophic writer so aptly puts it, "This inner functioning of cell and atom toward an evolutionary end, is not an argument for denial of the existence of a Supreme Creative Purpose, or God, but the best sustaining natural evidence for that existence.

"Thus the Supreme Creative Intelligence or Force must be, not only imminent in atom, cell and process, but must also trancend its creation. But imminence and trancendence are found only in what we call a *person*, that is, a self-referring subject of experience, that does not pass with its experience."

In the application of this Cosmic Concept to social organization it naturally follows that, "the most continuous permanent thing in creation is the demand of the human soul for freedom, the thirst for higher personal, spiritual and asthetic values.

When it comes to the ultimate,—the Origin of consciou-
sess—the materialist is even more at a loss. He claims that
'consciousness is the recognition, by the mind or ego, of
its own acts.'[2]

"Thus materialism fails to explain how consciousness
can arise from matter. Much less can it explain the origin
of consciousness, or the feeling of personal obligation to
do what is right. None of these problems can be explained
except by recognizing the fact of the indwelling presence
of the Spiritual Self, with its mind and conscience manifesting for a brief term of years, three-score-and-ten more
or less, through the animal organisms or body."[3]

These same objections apply to behaviorism and determinism. Behaviorism which ignores consciousness, is
but metaphysical materialism: while determinism is com-
pulsory materialism. Mere mechanics can never explain
organism, any more than mere analysis can explain life. It
ignores variety, spontaneity, and creation, all of which are
apparent in the universe.

CREATIVE HIERARCHIES:

All nature-forms are fashioned in the minds of the various Hierarchies of Builders or Creators, who are charged
with executing and manifesting the various types of ideas
in the Divine Mind. But as the substance of earth in which
those ideas and patterns must find expression, is so dense,
inert and unresponsive to the finer vibrations of the patterns, many imperfect and incomplete manifestations of
the basic idea or type,—the so-called misfits and failures
of Nature,—are manifested. Therefore the forms of Nature
are said to evolve or gradually approximate more and more
to the perfect expressions of the ideal of their type.

It is remembered that no piece of rock or stone is still,
and that all its particles are in movement orderly and con-

---

[2] *Twentieth Century Philosophy*, Flewelling.
[3] *Materialism*, Curtiss.

stant. It is only one step onward then, to realize that, in order for this movement to be maintained, there must be present some great force, a personality, of which it is the expression.

The whole material creation is nothing in itself and by itself. It is but the expression on a lower plane, of personalities on higher planes, the effects of which, their Wills are the causes. As a man leaves the imprint of his character on his work day by day, so these great Creative Lords and their ministers, have left the imprint of their personality on these material phenomena.

"Nothing is still; all moves continuously. This movement is controlled and orderly, and that is the warrant of the constant energizing of personality. As the lower grades of service are dependent on these Higher Lords for their existence and continuance, so these latter are to those of grades more sublime; as these are to the one Supreme Energy, the Self-Existent One, whose Will is our life, and Whose Wisdom is more wonderful than we can express in words or thoughts."[4]

BIBLICAL ILLUSTRATIONS:

This doctrine of the pre-existence of all things before they were materialized on Earth is taught in many Biblical passages. In Genesis ii, 5, we are told that God created "Every plant of the field before it was in the earth, and every herb of the field before it grew." And in St. John, viii, 58, we are told: "Verily, verily, I say unto you, before Abraham was I am." Again we read: "And now O Father, glorify thou me with thine own self, with the glory which I had with thee before the world was. . . . For thou lovedst me before the foundation of the world." (St. John, viii, 5). And this same doctrine is found in most world-religions and philosophies.

The point this chapter seeks to impress is that the higher, unseen worlds are not mere metaphysical abstractions, mental conceptions, or philosophic postulates, but are *real* worlds; just as real and just as variously inhabited as is the physical

---

[4] *Lowlands of Heaven*, Owen, 151.

world, but are composed of finer ethereal substances. In other words they are not mere subjective conceptions but *occupy actual position in space* and in relation to this physical world of form.[5]

SPIRIT ORIGIN:

Logic and these facts of all manifestation, force us to admit the fundamental thesis that back of all manifestation is spiritual causation, projection and animation.

In other words all manifestation is spirit-conceived, spirit-planned, spirit-formed, spirit-sustained, and spirit-projected, into the world of manifestation, and therefore man, in his spiritual nature is "little lower than the angels."

The poet Lowell must have had an intuitive realization of this truth even greater than he was conscious of, when he said. . . . "and beyond the dim unknown, standeth God within the shadows, keeping watch upon His own."

Modern science has abandoned the doctrine of materialism of the nineteenth century for that of dynamism or force, and this Cosmic Concept definitely refutes the claims of materialism, determinism and behaviorism, as theories of causation. It is only one step more in Science's expansion of consciousness to grasp the Cosmic Concept, and admit the Spiritual Origin of manifested Nature as well as man.

SCIENTISTS SAY:

Distinguished mathematicians assert that the Great Causeless Cause of all manifestation, or the Architect of the Universe, must be a Cosmic Mathematician, for all His laws which sustain the manifested expression of Nature, are capable of mathematical proof. Authorities in nuclear physics say that He must be a Cosmic Super Scientist, since the electrons within every atom circle around its central nucleus in orderly orbits corresponding to the orbits in which the planets circle around the sun.

---

[5] See diagrams in *Realms of the Living Dead*, Curtiss, 42.

Microscopists say that He must have an infinite and organizing Intelligence to co-ordinate the life activities of the swarms of infinitely minute organisms revealed in a drop of water, as exactly as they are in the grosser forms of life. In fact all living forms of Nature, minute or gigantic, give eloquent evidence that, back of all, there must be a Super-intelligent Intention, Plan, Purpose, Design, End-to-be-attained, and Will-to-manifest, which projects them all into material expression, animates them and maintains the harmonious, yet infinitely complex, "balance of Nature."

ILLUSTRATIONS:

For instance as we have pointed out elsewhere, there is the mud wasp—*Eumenes coarctate*—that plans far ahead for the nourishment of its progeny, which it never sees. It stings a caterpillar at the exact location of its cerebral nerve ganglion.

This paralyzes the caterpillar but keeps it alive until the wasp's eggs hatch out. The eggs are laid so that when the carnivorous grubs emerge they will have the fresh meat of a live carcass on which to feed.

But there is a still more remarkable instance of intelligence and farsighted planning in the case of the moth of the genus *Phonuba*. The female punctures the immature seed capsule of the *Yucca* flower and lays her eggs inside. She then pollenizes the stigma of the flower to insure that her nursery will be properly developed. Without this aid no seeds would be produced. Thus, by helping the plant to perpetuate its species she insures food for her young. These never know or contact their mother, for she is dead before they hatch.

INSTINCT:

To label all such manifestations of mind and intelligence "instinct" and then define that term as "an inherent impulse which incites men and other animals to those actions which are necessary for their guidance, preservation and development" is begging the question, for it does not explain the origin of the impulse and how it became inherent. The term "instinct" is merely a convenient name to cloak science's ignorance of the origin of the intelligence displayed. Where else could such long-range planning have originated, except in the spirit world of causation.

PROTOZOA:

But there is an even more astonishing manifestation of intelligence and discrimination. For example that found in the one-celled organism called *Protozoa*. These are so minute that it takes a high powered microscope even to see them. One such organism, *Didinium Nasutum*, which kills its prey by shooting poisonous, nettle-like darts into it, uses such volition, judgment and discrimination that it does not attack an object which is too large for it to kill and devour.

It will attack one species of *Animalcule* called the *Paramecium*, which is much larger than itself, yet it will not attack another species whose *ectoderm*, or skin, is too tough for the darts to penetrate.

These are facts that external conditions cannot determine; which are inexplicable by any mechanical theory. This is concept in strictest accord with the newest development of science, as it breaks with the materialistic, mechanistic theory, now so completely abrogated by scientific leaders everywhere. Evolution is not the mechanical reaction of outside forces, but is a true evolution, a development from within of a teleological or purposive, nature, of which human intelligence and moral achievement, are so far, the highest expression known to us.

To term these intelligent actions "trophisms" or "involuntary mechanical reactions to stimuli, light and chemicals, etc." is, again but the use of a convenient term to cover ignorance of why the reactions vary, and *why* they take place at all.

Whence comes this power of conscious choice, and delib-

erate discrimination? Again, where else could such manifestations of intelligence come from, except from the Spirit
World of Causation.

MATERIALISM FAILS:

What answer does *materialism* give to these problems?
And how satisfying is the answer? Materialism holds that
matter is the primordial or fundamental substance of the
universe, and that only matter and the forces generated
by it, are real; that the universe is not governed by intelligence, purpose or final causes, but only by haphazard
material causes.

Such materialism arises largely from the lack of early
training in religious facts, animal reactions only having
been explained.

Consequently the minds of persons lacking such training have great difficulty in appreciating the immaterial
facts of life, nature and consciousness. Since their whole
attention has been focused on material things, great self-
ishness develops, and they resent the knowledge that will
interfere with their self-indulgence.

The mental limitations of such ill-trained persons are
shown by the fact that while Nature surrounds them with
countless examples of plan, purpose, and design and the
will-to-manifest, from the beauty of design and the geo-
metrical perfection of the snowflake or the butterfly, to
the galaxies of universes majestically circling in their
appointed orbits, their minds are unable to see that back
of all the vast and intricate clockwork of manifestation,
there must be the Great Designer and Creator. Materialism,
therefore fails in explaining the Ultimate Cause of All,
which men call *God*.

SEVEN ULTIMATES:

As we have pointed out elsewhere, to be a comprehensive
philosophy, worthy of consideration, there are at least seven

ultimate questions, that a philosophy of life must answer. These must be satisfactorily answered, or that which is presented as a philosophy is only an incomplete theory or speculation.

The first ultimate that must be explained is the ultimate Cause of Manifestation; the second is the ultimate of the Origin of Life; the third is the Origin of Self-Consciousness; the fourth is the Object of Life; the fifth is the Reign of Law; the sixth is the Innate Instinct to Worship; and the seventh is the Ultimate End of Manifestation.

These ultimates can be answered in only one of two ways, either from the standpoint of materialism, or that of idealism or spiritualism, for we are necessarily either materialists or idealists.

BELIEF DOMINATES:

These ultimates *must* be answered because they are the basic questions which sooner or later clamor for explanation in every awakened mind that is living above the vegetative stage of animal consciousness, and has not been fossilized in a rut of materialistic doctrines, and closed to new ideas and concepts, by ignorance or narrow scientific and religious prejudice.

They must be answered because one's belief dominates his life. If we believe in God and our indwelling spiritual self, we live one way. If we believe that the universe is a mere mechanism for the blind expression of mechanical forces—chemical, electric, magnetic, solar etc.—we live in quite a different way.

If we believe that the Soul is immortal and manifests on earth through many incarnations, we naturally try to live so that our next incarnation will be a great improvement over this one. On the other hand if we believe that we are merely, "a fortuitous agglomeration of invisible chemical elements"; that mind is but a chemical activity of the cells of the brain, and that the death of the body ends all, we live a life of animal indulgence, or a bleak, despondent life, without hope or incentive to progress, and with little joy in living. But if we believe in our personal survival after death, our belief gives meaning to every effort we make for spiritual advance.

"Life is not the result of organization, but organization is the result of life. All organized entities, whether spiritual or material, are secondary to the life principle within them. The pressure of life seeking expression in matter, is the cause of evolution. Matter and spirit are co-existent and co-equal; one is the passive and the other is the active principle in Nature. But the God principle is active to both."[6]

PERSONALISM:

Personalism according to Bronson Alcott is "the doctrine that the ultimate reality of the world is a Divine Person, who sustains the universe by a continuous act of creative Will."[7]

One spirit communicator from the Higher Realms has truly said, "I do not understand all the processes, but I do know that for an ungraspably infinite period, the individual man, created in the image of the consciousness that has reached man's estate here, will go on as an individual. 'God made man in His own image.'. . . Human consciousness, the height of individualized consciousness, reveals itself in a form that is a copy of the actuality which is the consciousness itself."[8]

And again; "Filling all space is a great sea of undifferentiated force; we can call it life or spirit, or the Universal. . . . But it is the thing, by virtue of which all living things exist, through their ability to transmute this general force into something individual. In other words we are all vital transformers. It follows that we are alive and developed in proportion to how much of this force we can accept, and how freely it flows through us. The better we do this the higher

---

[6] *Immortality*, Peebles, 93.
[7] *Pedler's Progress*, Shephard, 494.
[8] *Unobstructed Universe*, White.

grade we occupy, and the more alive and contented and effective we become."[9]

There is ultimate satisfaction for the individual and the solution of his problem, only in the realization of his Spiritual Self (Personalism) a living philosophy because it is a philosophy of life. The highest can only be achieved by spiritual realization, for moral values are the most real.

As Flewelling says in *Twentieth Century Philosophy*, page 339; "The values of good-will and love do not need to be argued anywhere. The beauty of self-forgetfulness for the common good is recognized in every religion."

This complete realization of the unity and oneness of all things can come only by the subjugation of animal self-ishness, and the individual interests, or in the sublimation of all interests to the highest and supreme values of life.

Personalism, as has been well said, includes; "its re-lationship to new scientific discovery, its provision for meeting the exigencies of a changing world of thought, its outlook on education, its provision for religious interests, and its necessity to a surviving democracy. In all the his-tory of philosophic and scientific thought the world has not been faced by so complete and so significant a reversal of opinion since the days of Copernicus. In the space of thirty years, we have had the most revolutionary discoveries; Radio-Activity, the doctrine of the Relativity of Space and Time, the Quantum Theory, the discovery of the Atomic Force, to mention but a few. These discoveries indicate the passing of scientific materialism, which has held sway for so long, to the exclusion of the higher personal and aesthetic values."[10]

REALITY:

All reality is, in some sense, personal, and there are only personalities of various degrees of creative power, and what they create. Personality is self-conscious and self-directive,

---

[9] *Across the Unknown*, White, 23.
[10] *Twentieth Century Philosophy*, Flewelling, 334-5.

both in finite individuals, and in the Supreme Creative Intelligence, which is the world Basis and Source of all Reality. Personality is thus the very essence of being, the super individuality of spirit; is the fundamental Real which finds the expression of itself through the mind. Even Divine Mind therefore, is not the Real, the Source of all,—though creating all,—or God. For back of mind there must be Consciousness which finds expression in concrete thought forms, in the mind; thought forms so concrete that they have frequently been photographed. Back of the Consciousness there must be the Ideation, which functions through Consciousness, and back of the Ideation there must be the Ideal or the Thinker and Creator Himself, Who is ever seeking expression through these various aspects of Himself, in the various worlds of manifestation.

It is from this Primal Source that mind derives its creative power and its ability to differentiate itself from the objective world, and its own creations and experiences. This Law of Divine Reality is the fundamental principle of permanence, in the various worlds of manifestation where all is change.

"Reality can no longer be conceived as something out there in which the person has no part or lot. What is 'out there' is also a function of what is 'in here.'"[11]

CONSCIOUSNESS:

There exists in you indefinitely developable, an engine of power, dynamically creative, capable of impressing and molding your material world, according as you give out from your inner being its creative force. This force is not primarily the *mentally* creative force which you understand perfectly. It is the higher sense of that mentally creative force, the vital principle of life, and comes, *not* from that mere agent of the soul, the intellect, but from the very plexus of life itself. The mental force can make a mold or plan, but for completion this plan must have its vital principle supplied.

---

[11] *Twentieth Century Philosophy*, Flewelling, 334.

Consciousness is the one and only Reality, whether it be the lower consciousness or the Higher Consciousness. That of which we are conscious, exists for us. The Higher Consciousness is the desire to reach the highest in individual perception of the Great Consciousness, or God; it is harmonious adjustment to It in understanding and realization. This Higher Consciousness must not be thought of as something *still* within us, something which we get and hold, but as a continually moving current, and is of no value if we *contain* it only, and do not let it flow through us, and share it with the world. It is like taking food into our bodies and retaining all of it. We become so clogged that serious congestion and ill-health result.

So it is with the taking of the Higher Consciousness. We must keep open the channels of outgo as well as those of intake. And as an invisible whose consciousness extends from the other side tells us. "The way to make room for more is to use more. And draining out for use establishes suction for the flowing in. Our output is actually the measure of our intake."[12]

"Therefore the great secret of all progress, is to let the Universal Force continually flow through you as often as possible to clear moments in your life in which to circulate it intensively through your being, stimulating your mind and body, and every part of you; and then, nourished by it, to let your mental faculties plan its utilization.

"Keep constantly in mind the powerhouse idea, making sure you possess its feeling of strength, before attempting to distribute—or combat. Minimize your sensitiveness, your susceptibility to adverse influences; and work on maintaining your force by keeping it in constant association with the powerhouse."[13]

---

[12] *Across the Unknown*, White, 221.
[13] *Across the Unknown*, White, 314.

Spiritualism:

What is spiritualism, and in this all important study of Cosmic Philosophy and its relation to man in a personal sense, what part does spiritualism play?

Arthur Ford in a broadcast from Miami, Florida, gives a splendid answer to this very relevant and important question, and to its relationship to Cosmic Philosophy:

"Literally, spiritualism is the antithesis of materialism. . . . Every person is either a spiritualist or a materialist. . . . He believes, either that there is a spiritual quality in him, which survives physical death, or that death is the end of it all, and only the things that matter are the things of time and sense. . . . Spiritualism relies on observation. . . . its method is scientific. Spiritualism has an important and compelling message for humanity at a time when chaos, death and destruction stalk across the world. . . . In the face of the stark realities of war, what a boon it is to know that there is one thing that is beyond the power of death, and that human personality survives all the destructive forces loosed upon the earth.

"Spiritualism stresses the supreme value of human personality. It puts the emphasis exactly where Jesus did, and where all the great redemptive teachers of the race have put it, upon the eternal supremacy of the soul. But it also says that the whole question of the intrinsic worth of the individual can be taken out of the realm of pious belief, or poetic sentiment and placed upon a scientific basis.

"It says that there is abundant proof that God prizes personality far too highly ever to let it be wholly lost. It knows that the most backward people, as well as those who boast of their superior culture, must go on after death whether they want to or not.

"It knows that life after death is lived in accordance with the law of cause and effect; that what we sow here we shall reap there; and that the moral values of life hold inexorably.

"Having a factual basis for this belief, no spiritualist could be guilty of racial or religious prejudices. These twin evils, which have been, and are, causing so much strife and bitterness in the world, are alien to everything we have learned from those exalted ones who speak to us from the spirit side of life.

"Believing as we do that all life is the manifestation of one Infinite Intelligence, we refuse to be a party to any form of bigotry or intolerance.

"Spiritualism believes that the proof it offers, relative to man's nature, will make inevitable a revival of the importance of *mind* and *spirit* in the natural order, where too often in the past the tendency has been to see only *force* and *matter*.

"This is fundamental to any high idealism, as it means a larger universe than that perceived by our senses; not in a quantitative sense, but in a qualitative sense, where faith, hope and love and aspiration have as real a place as eyes and hands; a real universe in which ideal things have an actual existence.

"If our claims are true, and should they gain wide acceptance, it will have far greater power to uphold moral agencies, and inspire moral striving, than had the belief in immortality based simply on faith, for it will possess an efficacy that can never attach to a belief not so assured and buttressed by facts.

"In such a universe God and all the meanings attached to that name, become vivid and real."[14]

We quote again from Stewart Edward White's splendid book *The Unobstructed Universe*, pages 37, 64.

"Next is your realization of what your scientists have admitted, that there exists in the only one universe of which you are a part, much that your senses cannot detect, but which have been proved to exist by means of instruments invented by man.

"Recognition of the Creator as greater than the thing created. . . . acceptance of the Oneness of Consciousness as a whole. . . . is the rock strong enough to support the many-

[14] See *Harbinger of Light*, Oct. 1st, 1945.

storied and various superstructure that to-day's science has
made ours. Realization that man's thoughts and their effect on the whole, as well as on himself; not only here and
now in his own little segment of the universe, but on out
in an eternal continuity; immortality! not as some vague
and distant possibility, but you . . . . here . . . . now! this is
the thing that you must recapture, as an intimate working
principle."

To sum up, reality is an activity towards ends, and
needs. The person himself, his welfare, physical, mental,
and spiritual; his opportunity for development, consonant
with the rights and freedom of others, is the end of all
statecraft or social organization.

As Raivasson says, "Something more than includes all
is to found in personality, which since it unifies all the
diversities into a unity, is reality itself. Unity in space is
organization, in time it is life, where individuality begins.
Life is not only organization, it is self-organization."[15]

Infinity is unconditioned, unlimited, and unrelated;
hence we can grasp only some of its manifestations. The
universe and its Creator are Infinite, hence they cannot be
fully grasped by our three dimensional minds.

"That the world of *things* springs from an intelligent
Source must of necessity be realized by all normal minds,
and human perceptions as true. The moral laws are held
to be as inexorable in their outworkings as any other law
of Nature. The Cosmic Order, being personal, is also ethi-
cal, and the moral mandates are written into the nature of
things."[16]

And so we find that; "That is no such thing as blind
or unconscious force in all God's Kingdom of Creation.
Not a ray of light, not an impulse of heat, not an electrical
wave proceeds from your sun or any other star, but is the
effect of a cause; and that cause is a conscious cause; it is
the Will of some conscious Being energizing in a certain
and positive direction."[17]

---

[15] *Twentieth Century Philosophy*, Flewelling, 331-2.
[16] *Unobstructed Universe*, White.
[17] *The Lowlands of Heaven*, Owen, 144.

CHAPTER II

PROBLEM OF INCARNATION

To understand death fully we must in turn have an understanding of life and the processes of incarnation.

THE OBJECT OF LIFE:

When it comes to explaining the reason for, and the *object of life*, the materialist holds that it is merely for the organism to maintain itself, and reproduce its kind. If that idea were true there would be no incentive, or even impulse, to strive for progress or any higher attainment. Life on such a basis would be an utterly selfish struggle for creature comforts and the indulgence of the senses and the appetites of the flesh. That such a sordid idea is not true is proved by the fact that a scientific study of the processes of all organic life shows that it is a purposive, creating evolution, progressing toward an intelligent and definite goal.

The purely mechanistic conception of life is also disproved by the fact that we find mankind hungering for the immaterial things of the Spirit, such as freedom, justice, wisdom and love. Man is also altruistically willing to sacrifice his life for his country, for a cause in which he believes, or for one whom he loves. Such qualities cannot be produced, either by chemical activity or by mere organic functioning. Since a stream cannot rise higher than its source, such high ideals must have their origin in a source far higher than the physical.

MATERIALIZATION OF IDEALS:

Only the student of spiritual science can have a fully satisfactory explanation of the object of life here on earth. For he knows that every form of life is but an imperfect materialisation of the ideal of that form which has been projected from the mind of God, for embodiment in matter. The object of all life is therefore *the manifestation of the ideal*. Since this is the universal *Law of Manifestation* in Nature it applies to man as well as to the lower kingdoms. For man, the Real or Spiritual Man, the Adam of the first chapter of *Genesis*, was also created in the higher unseen worlds long before the physical vehicle for his manifestation on Earth, the animal body mentioned in the second chapter of *Genesis* as having been not *created* but *formed* out of the dust of the ground, had been evolved for his use.[1]

In man this ideal is the pre-existing, super-physical and super-mortal Spiritual Self. The object of life is to respond to, and express more and more of this Spiritual Self.

However much the individual may misunderstand his own needs, and abuse his best opportunities, there is satisfaction for him at long last, and the solution of his problems only in the realization of his best and highest self.

As we have said before, when a potter starts to make a wonderful vase,—a marvel of beauty, a poem of symbology, a lesson for all who look,—he does not copy something another mind has brought forth. Such a production would be an imitation of the real. The true potter, the artist, is original. Long before one stroke is made, even before the clay is moistened, his mind has created every detail of the vase.[2]

As long as we regard ourselves as mere mortals, death will have all the terrors of the unknown. But once we realize that we are immortal souls, who have reincarnated many times, and therefore have experienced many deaths, death is but a

---

[1] For details see *The Truth About Evolution and the Bible*, Curtiss, 55.
[2] *The Voice of Isis*, Curtiss, 306.

beneficent incident in the cycle of immortal life. This understood dispels all the fears and terrors of death.

DEATH A VICTORY:

Properly understood death can be a victorious experience in life everlasting, a joyous dropping-off of all the limitations and bondages of the flesh. It can be a triumphant entrance into a greater realization of life eternal in the heavenly realms; the consummation of a long awaited, universal and inevitable experience in immortal life.

OUR TRUE HOME:

The reference to pre-existence given in Chapter 1 are enough to establish the fact that the Earth is not our true home or place of origin, and that our Real or Spiritual Self, is an individualized, spiritual being, who exists, independent of, and superior to, its limited expression through our human animal-body.

In other words, our Spiritual Self is an individualized Ray of God, projected into the worlds of form to manifest the potencies and powers of God. Just as the rays of the sun are individualized expressions of the sun, every beam of which contains all the potencies and powers of the sun, projected for embodiment into all the living forms of Nature, just so are we Rays of the Spiritual Sun, containing all its potencies and powers. Hence we are properly called "Sons of God."

"We are gods" was not said in a mere figurative sense. Man may become a god or that which has all the magnitude and grandure of a god, as we are told in "Letters from a Living Dead Man," Barker.

It is this Spiritual Self which is now commonly recognized by psychologists and psychiatrists as limiting our reactions, and is referred to as the "mentor" or "censor."

And as the ancient Hindu teachings put it, "Man is a Crystal Ray: a Beam of Light, immaculate within a form of clay material upon the lower surface. That Beam is thy Life Guide and thy True Self; the Watcher and the Silent Thinker, the victim of the lower self." [3]

PARENTS CHOSEN:

To accomplish this, when we come into incarnation, we usually choose parents with whom we have set up strong karmic ties in past lives, or those who will give us the type of body and brain,—not mind, for we bring our own mind with us,—and the environment which, from our soul's outlook, we see will be best suited to teach us the needed lessons, even though the life chosen might appear rugged and harsh to the personality. We choose our life from the standpoint of the object to be accomplished, not for the conveniences or pleasures of the personality.

PLANE OF DEMONSTRATION:

Since the Earth-Plane is the Plane of Demonstration, one reason why we come down to earth from our home in the heaven-worlds, is to learn and demonstrate the lessons necessary to complete the manifestation of our Spiritual Self, through the body of flesh in this lowest world of matter.

On some occasions we incarnate only temporarily, when it is not our cycle or full life term, to divert the chosen parents from a frivolous life of social striving, mere money making, or other material ends, and turn them to the study of Spiritual Truths. The early death of a beloved babe often diverts the parents' life, and leads them to seek the Path of Spiritual Attainment. On such occasions the parents sometimes remain in close touch with, and are responsive to, the guiding influence of such a child after its passing over.

Before reincarnating we usually estimate about how long it will take us to accomplish our life's plan, and so come prepared to stay an approximate number of years, upon the conclusion of which, we withdraw. This life-term may be voluntarily shortened by war, suicide, accident, or improper living,

[3] *The Voice of the Silence*, Blavatsky, Fragment 111.

or it may be lengthened by some strong desire for some worthwhile accomplishment.

ACCOMPLISHMENT:

As we have previously stated, the main object of incarnation is to afford the Spiritual Self an opportunity to manifest in the flesh all the spiritual qualities which It has acquired, and the degree of their unfoldment here on earth, as it has already done in the higher worlds. To accomplish its life mission, our Spiritual Self must have a responsive physical instrument through which It can contact, respond to, and utilize physical conditions. Naturally this greatly limits the expression of its life and consciousness, but it is the best It can do under the circumstances. The body is therefore, often a most hampering and rebellious instrument, for the animal-self has desires and a will of its own, which must ultimately be made subservient to the desires and will of the Spiritual Self, until it is willing to say to that Self, "not my will but Thine be done."

St. Paul recognizes this fundamental conflict when he says, "I delight after the Law of God *after the Inner Man*, but I see another law in my members, warring against the law of my mind, and bringing me into captivity to the law of sin."[4]

CAUSE AND EFFECT:

This shows that God neither rewards nor punishes us but gives us free will to follow His guidance. He allows His great Law of Cause and Effect to operate in the Higher Worlds as in this world, so we have no one to blame for our after-death conditions but ourselves. Do not blame God when you reap the results of your own creations through the vibrations you have generated, and the causes you have set in motion, for we reward and punish ourselves by reaping the results of the conditions we have created in this earth life. It is a sacrilege to think of a God of love and justice condemning

---

[4] *Romans*, vii, 22.

us to eternal punishment for mistakes made, largely through ignorance, while in one short earth life. This realization removes the great fear-complex generated through ages of misunderstanding of the allegorical nature of the Biblical descriptions of the conditions of the after life.

OUR REWARDS:

Persons who held high positions in this world, and were possessors of much of this world's goods, but who developed little love, compassion or spirituality, will find themselves poverty stricken in the world of spirit. On the other hand those of lowly position on earth, and with perhaps little of this world's goods, but who have highly developed characters and spiritual qualities, will find themselves surrounded in the hereafter by conditions of love, light, happiness and progress.

This law is aptly illustrated in the reversed positions of the beggar Lazarus and the rich man—St. Luke, xvi, 19-25—for in the after-life it was the rich man who cried from torment, begging help from Lazarus, reposing in the "bliss of Abraham's bosom."

One writer tells us in a message he received from the other side; "While all are clothed in the spirit-world, only those are clothed in crystal whiteness who have *overcome*; overcome their passions and their earthly appetites, in the sense of training and subordinating them to divine uses. Clothing in the spirit-world corresponds to character. Many of the proud and costly attired of earth will find themselves so spiritually nude and poor in the world of spirit, that they will feel to compare their vestures to filthy rags." Swedenborg, by far the greatest seer of the last century, describes it thus, "Many of the learned of earth are amazed when they find themselves, after death, in houses, in bodies and in garments much as those of earth."[5]

Since we have described in more detail, in our *Realms of the Living Dead* the clothing worn, the methods of feeding,

---

[5] *Immortality*, Peebles, 61-2.

the transportation, and the various occupations followed in the after-life, we refer you to that volume for further details.

DIVER'S SUIT:

The body may therefore be likened to the cumbersome suit of a diver, with its great dome helmet and heavily weighted boots, which the diver must don in order to work on the bottom of the ocean. Although this greatly hampers his activities, it is the best he can do under the conditions. But to accomplish even this limited work, he must keep in touch with the upper world of light and air, through the life line and the air tube, or he could not continue to function below.

Likewise to accomplish its mission, the incarnated Soul must keep in touch with the Higher Worlds through the Life Ray, and continue to breathe the "Breath of Heaven" through spiritual aspiration, or It will be cut off from its Source and become a soulless animal.

AN OVERCOAT:

Using another simile, the hampering conditions of the body may be likened to a cumbersome overcoat which it is necessary for us to wear to manifest through the storms of winter. But when we return *home* we lay aside this hampering garment, and thus are free to accomplish many activities which we were unable to do while bundled up in it. We can also ascend to a higher story in our home, from which vantage point, we can see farther out and get a more comprehensive view of outer conditions, than we could while on the ground floor. We may liken "death" to taking off our overcoat and ascending one flight higher up.

WE REMAIN UNCHANGED:

Just as taking off our overcoat and going upstairs does not immediately alter our character, disposition or desires, so taking off our garment of flesh does not alter them either. We remain the same personality and in the same degree of evolution as we were before laying aside the body of flesh, *until we have progressed beyond* those conditions while in the higher realms.

SPIRITUALITY SOUGHT:

So the latest scientific evidence shows that laying aside the physical body, does not at once greatly alter the living, which seems to be but a continuation of the interests and pursuits we had while on earth, until they are outgrown, satisfied or transmuted.

Ordinarily we ascend automatically to the realms to which our vibrations of thought, character, and associations affinitize us. If our main thoughts and desires are still centered on earth conditions, they naturally hold us and keep us close to earth, "earth-bound" until we graduate from that grade and go higher.

So death does not automatically confer spirituality. That attribute must still be achieved, through aspiration and growth, in the Higher Realms, just as surely as it must be while on earth. The attainment of the Christ Consciousness or Cosmic Consciousness, must still be sought for and the needed growth reached as persistently in these Higher Realms as it was on the earth plane.

In other words, taking off our overcoat of flesh does not make us "bright and shining angels" all at once.

HEAVENLY SURROUNDINGS:

As the law of Cause and Effect "whatsoever a man soweth, that shall he also reap," is in effect in the higher realms as well as on Earth, in the higher worlds we find ourselves surrounded by the exact conditions we have created while on earth, by our thoughts, emotions, words and deeds. Thus we are furnishing our heavenly home here and now. This is referred to by Jesus when he said. "In my Father's house are many mansions. . . . that where I am there ye may be also." John, iv, 2-3.

How shocking must thy summons be, O Death!
To him that is at ease in his possessions;
Who, counting on long years of pleasure here.
Is quite unfurnished for that world to come.

The Grave, BLAIR

If our main interest in life has been in music, we naturally gravitate to the realm where music and musical pursuits predominate. If interested in art we naturally join other art lovers. If our chief interest has been religion, we go to the regions where religious ceremonies are held. If our desires have been of a low nature, we are inevitably attracted to the region peopled by those of similar low desires, and so on downward to the lowest slums of the Astral World, where such evil conditions prevail, which are commonly referred to as "hell."

But we cannot too often repeat that all persons do not have to pass through the hell conditions, any more than they have to live in slums on earth. It is only those who are affinitized to these low conditions by their own thoughts, desires, and actions who have to experience them.

And let us repeat, the thing to keep clearly in mind is that *your body is not you*. It is only an outer garment of flesh which you put on in order that you may contact the physical conditions of Earth-life, while you remain essentially the same as you were until you progress, in consciousness.

Heaven and hell are therefore, not only states of mind, but are regions as tangible to our spirit-body as the regions of earth are to our physical body.

We cannot too often repeat that your body is only your "house" or dwelling place; your overcoat or shell which you discard when you go through the gateway of this "thing called death." You use it while you are on this earth plane, to gain the experiences of that plane for the benefit of your Soul's growth.

Modern psychic research shows that the poet Holland was correct when he wrote:

"Heaven is not reached by a single bound;
But we climb the ladder by which we rise.
From the lowly earth to the vaulted skies.
And we mount to its summit round by round."

CHAPTER III

PROBLEM OF REINCARNATION

No philosophy that purports to explain the circumstances of life, with their inconsistencies, contradictions, inequalities, seeming injustices, unmerited suffering and apparent success of evil, can give a satisfactory explanation of these conditions, without including the facts of reincarnation. Life cannot be explained without including this law. Reincarnation is therefore the only answer to humanity's eternal cry of why? why? why?

A CHRISTIAN DOCTRINE:

As we have treated this subject somewhat extensively as well as scientifically elsewhere, we herein give only a brief outline of the law. In doing so we feel that we are on safe ground theologically, as well as scientifically, for Jesus taught specifically that John the Baptist was a reincarnation of Elias when he said; "Elias shall first come and restore all things. But I say unto you *that Elias is already come*, and they knew him not." St. Matthew, vii, 11-12. And again; "If you will receive it *this is Elias* which was for to come." Mark, xvii, 10. The fact that John denied that he was Elias—John, i, 21.[1]—merely proves that we do not ordinarily remember our past incarnations, as we are now using an entirely new brain, furnished by our parents, within which no vibrations of the past are recorded.

---

[1] See also—St. Mark, vi, 15.—St. Mathew, xvi. 13-14.—St. John, ix, 2.—St. Matthew, xvi, 17.—St. John, iii, 3-10.—St. Matthew, xii, 41-42.—Acts, xv, 16.—Revelations, iii, 12.—St. John, viii, 53-54.

THE LAW IGNORED:

Although this law was well known to the early church fathers, it has been pointedly ignored by theologians of later ages, for its acceptance would necessitate the revision of their materialization of the allegories of a lake of fire, brimstone, and eternal punishment, used to describe the after-death suffering and mental torment of remorse for evil deeds, and the disentegrating effects of the evil we have created, which constitute the only hell-fire and torment. The fact of the existence of the materialization of an actual lake of fire, and eternal punishment after death, has now been scientifically disproved and no such literal condition has been discovered, in even the lowest slums or hell-regions of the astral world. Therefore the bogies of fear of eternal punishment, which is so frequently used to coerce men's minds to accept their theological dogmas no longer holds water among independent thinkers who have investigated the problem.

The removal of this incubus of fear of eternal punishment, for temporary mistakes or evils, is one of the greatest accomplishments of psychical research for the freedom of the hearts and minds of mankind. Through reincarnation the soul can learn and adjust the results of the suffering it has inflicted in the past on others, by having corresponding experiences of its own in this life, until the Christ spirit is sufficiently realized to be able to "forgive Its enemies."

CYCLIC MANIFESTATION:

It is well known that all manifestation is cyclic. First there is a period of activity and outgoing into manifestation, in which the events of the day are experienced. Then there is a period of withdrawal into sleep and rest, while the experiences of the "day" are digested.

Then there is the larger period of the summer, in which the seeds sprout, buds open and growth and fruition result. This is followed by the fall and winter season, during which all manifestations of the summer's life are withdrawn, and the results of the season's growth are solidified into sturdy wood, upon which the next season's manifestation will take place. Since it is obvious that one day's existence is not sufficient for the development and expression of one's character, and one summer's growth is not sufficient for the complete manifestation of a giant tree, but that many nights and winters must intervene, just so is it obvious that one incarnation is not sufficient for the complete unfoldment and expression of the Spiritual Self through the garment of flesh. Each incarnation is but one school day, or summer period, in the life of the soul, with many winter periods of death and disembodiment intervening, during which intervals the Soul assimilates the experiences of the incarnation and builds them into Soul growth, with which to begin the next incarnation. To the average untrained individual, death is the end of all human relationships. This is not true as we have seen, for as sleep is a short interval between our experiences of Earth conditions, to the consciousness of which we "die" nightly, so death is only a longer interval of rest and recuperation between incarnations into earthly conditions.

Hence, just as surely as we awaken each morning and bring back with us all that we have learned in previous days, just so surely will we survive and awaken into a new day—period of life, in the next incarnation, bringing with us as inherent faculties, all the gains we have made in the last life, together with all we have learned in the higher realms, between death and rebirth, as stock in trade, with which to start the new incarnation.

Birth and death are therefore as inevitable as day and night, summer and winter, which mark the cyclic changes in the material manifestation of Nature, but obviously these changes do not mark the end of life.

INBORN QUALITIES:

The only portion of goods with which the Father endows His prodigal son for his long sojourn in this far country of

Earth embodiment is the character, traits and accomplishments which he brings with him as inborn qualities. These qualities are so powerful that they modify the physical heredity which our parents give to the body. Thus even tiny infants exhibit decided traits of character which differentiate them markedly from other children of the same family, long before they are able to talk. Materialists say that these are "inborn propensities," but fail to say why they are inborn and whence they came. Since God cannot fairly be accused of being so unfair and partial as to make one personality a genius, and another equally innocent babe a moron, obviously the only answer to the unbending law of cause and effect is that the character and traits must have been earned by the Soul, through the slow law of growth in a past life.

They are therefore born into the new personality as inborn traits and attainments, with which to start this new day-period in the school of Earth-life.

If heredity and environment, were, as claimed by the materialists and determinists, the deciding factors formulating personality, all children of the same parents and brought up in the same environment would be as much alike as peas in a pod, which obviously they are not.

BONDS OF CONNECTION:

Remember that while love is the strongest bond of association which brings souls together in the new incarnation, hatred is the next strongest. Therefore be sure that you do not pass out of this life filled with antagonism or hatred, or you will very likely be incarnated in close contact, perhaps in the same family, with the one thus hated, until the hate is neutralized and worked out. This could scarcely be done if you had a clear memory of the previous life.

This explains sudden and unreasoning attraction, or repulsion, for people whom you have met for the first time, and for which there is no apparent cause. It is like old friends or enemies suddenly meeting face to face, after a long absence.

In exceptional cases, however, a person who is suddenly cut off in the midst of youth,—as in battle or accident,—may reincarnate within a few months to fill out the balance of the last life. During World War I we had one student who reincarnated through the same mother, within a few months after his graduation into the higher life. Naturally the mother had to be open to the astral, as do all mothers, to make the incarnation possible, but in this case she was so open and responsive that she knew who it was who wished to incarnate, so that when he was born, she gave him the same name, the same room, the same playthings, etc. that he had before. In fact many mothers sense the character of the Soul who is incarnating, even though they may not exactly recognize who it is.

UNINFORMED GUIDES:

Some spiritualists say that they do not believe in reincarnation, as their "guides" say that they know nothing of it in the after-life. This is easily explained, for since the guides and their friends were not interested in the subject while on earth, it is only natural that they would associate with those on the other side of life who also knew nothing about it.

In our years of research we have encountered a number of such guides, who said they knew nothing of the subject, but who were open-minded enough to investigate it, at our suggestion, with the teachers in the Higher Realms. In each case their researches completely satisfied them of the truth, and from then on they taught it in their séances.

TESTIMONY OF SIR OLIVER LODGE:

Since this law has recently been confirmed from the higher side of life by the great scientist Sir Oliver Lodge, after four years of intensive investigation, since passing to the Higher Realms, and since the subject is now being favorably discussed in spiritualistic magazines, it is fitting that a brief reference to it be included herein.

This noted scientist and investigator says; "I have delayed making this statement so that I could be sure, to my own satisfaction, that I am giving you the correct deductions; that I am giving you facts founded on the observations I have made since my transition. During this Earth life I have kept an open mind on this vexed subject on what is *called reincarnation. . . . Well, now I know that it is a fact. It is true. . . .* According to my personal experience, it is true."[2] This testimony of so eminent a scientist and authority, after years of posthumous investigation, together with the mass of other evidence and physical proof, should be sufficient to convince any open mind of this law as a fact in Nature, and not a mere convenient theory.

FREEWILL:

Many say that this life is so difficult that they have no desire to come back again, but they are judging from the limited mortal viewpoint of the personality, and not from the Soul's standpoint. As a matter of fact, since they still have freewill, they will not have to come back until they so desire, even though they remain out of incarnation for ages. But ultimately they will realize that they cannot progress further without returning to the Earth plane of demonstration. We encountered one guide who claimed she had been out of incarnation since the days of ancient Lemuria, more than 30,000 years ago. We do not doubt her claim as she was teaching the same old concepts as she then taught, instead of reincarnating many times and progressing, and attaining a greater consciousness and wider outlook, in each incarnation.

As we have shown therefore, we reincarnate to demonstrate the character, talents and skills we have developed in previous lives, that we may continue to improve them, until we have attained God-Consciousness. After this has been attained, we will have to "go no more out" into incarnation, as the Bible tells us in Revelation, iii, 12, unless we desire, out

---

[2] *Psychic News*, Sept. 8th, 1945.

of love and compassion to return as teachers or leaders, to help our less evolved fellow men.

Reincarnation is a logical sequence of the continuity of the life of the Soul apart from the physical body, and properly understood, with the Law of Karma, reveals to man the eternal nature of life.

A very high spirit teacher, White Eagle gives us the following from the other side.

"When a man is once convinced of the continuity of life, when he can see that through reincarnation there can be revealed a wide and grand purpose in all life's experiences, it gives him hope, not only for the future, but for the present. It gives him a reason for many of life's happenings.

"Life's purpose begins to reveal itself. He sees that the soul travels a journey which commenced when it was *breathed-forth* from the heart of God; and, descending through the spheres of spiritual life, came to the earth to gain experiences; to gain consciousness. . . .

"Through this process of succeeding incarnations it gains *quality of consciousness*—eventually such a rich quality that it becomes *God-Conscious*. . . . We are well aware that people try to argue against this teaching of the *Ancient Wisdom*. . . . Neither argument nor opinion can alter truth. Sooner or later he who argues against this truth, will be for it; he will suddenly know that he has lived on this earth before. Once the *soul attains* this super-conscious state, memories flood in upon it.

"By studying humanity you will find that there are many people unable to understand even elementary spiritual truth. They may be intellectual and clever, but still incapable of seeing, hearing, or comprehending anything spiritual in spite of their ability and so-called common sense.

"In other words, they lack the quality of consciousness, or the ripeness of consciousness, which alone can give them comprehension.

"Many others require no argument, they do not need to be

convinced of spiritual truth; it is already there in them; they are born with it.

"The quality of consciousness which the soul brings back into incarnation depends entirely on the life which preceded it. When this quality is developed it will naturally and normally be spiritual in its nature, with knowledge of the life after death.

"Such souls do not regard such a procedure as a succession of incarnations as objectionable or in any way retrogressive, but see it revealed as a path of eternal progress; they will see that as the soul returns to each successive life it bears with it a richer quality of consciousness,— which by the way, can only be attained by the everyday experiences, suffering and hard work of physical life. . . .

"A strange thing is that every other person, who believes in reincarnation claims to have once been either a king or queen, or some other notable historical character. Such memories or such statements originate because of the pride in the individual. We cannot all have been great, true; but we do know that it is sometimes necessary for souls who once held a position of power to reincarnate subsequently in very humble positions.

"We know also that people who lived in obscure conditions wisely, truly, and honorably prepare themselves for a subsequent incarnation which affords them greater dignity, power and opportunity to serve mankind.

"The whole purpose of reincarnation is for the development and training of the soul. It must learn how to use power wisely and humbly; it must learn how to accept with simplicity and humility the limitations which it has earned before it can find the truth concerning itself.

"Some souls who pass to the spirit world apparently escape retribution for their sins and short comings. They appear to live in comfort and happiness much as many people dwell comfortably and complacently down here on earth. . . .

"Their past actions and how they affect the whole community apparently bothers them not at all; but, consider,— whatever a man soweth in laziness and complacency, in indifference to the sufferings of others, he will experience himself. Perhaps not in this incarnation, perhaps not in the spirit world during his soul's period of rest, or in the intermediary state between one life and another; but *as sure as night follows day, men, races and nations meet that which they have meted out to others, either by active evil or cruelty through neglect*, which latter might be called inactive cruelty.

"But perhaps your experience may not necessarily re- sult from either action or reaction, but because of neglect of opportunity. This is a strange saying, but suffering and disappointment often offer opportunity to the soul. Once the soul knows this, it will accept its lesson with humility, will not question and will not demand to know why. By its quality of consciousness gained, it has either repaid a debt, or earned the opportunity to expand.

"Do you not see what such an understanding of life's principles as this, means to men and women? It means inward peace, it means assured happiness deep within; it means complete trust and faith in God's love and God's wisdom; in the wise laws which control the universe, and which control the *Life of Man*; which commenced with the birth of the soul aeons ago, and came to fruition when the soul stands forth a perfect God-man. . . .

"We tell you that reincarnation is no weary round of birth and death. After touching the high spheres of light and glory, an exorable law does not force the reluctant soul back to the dull drab conditions of physical life. No— *something far more beautiful happens*. The soul after death passes onward into a state of light and peace, and there is able to review itself.

"Do you know what the soul instinctively yearns for when it sees its past in due perspective?—it cries. '*Oh, my God, for another chance! I will do better—next time*.'' Is this not logical?

"How few of us fail to look back over our years and say

that if only we had our time over again what different lives we would lead! God in His mercy offers such another opportunity to the soul.

"In the old Masonic phrasing 'the soul comes forth to labor on the earth; but it returns to its true home, to its true self for refreshment; then again it returns to labor.'

"This ancient teaching is a profound truth. Its acceptance should add much beauty to life, bring to you all encouragement and an inward happiness; because you will then know that however simple, however limited your life may be, everything will be worth while; because life provides you with opportunities to grow, to be educated, to continually develop this glorious quality of soul-consciousness which will eventually reveal truth and God.

"*Life's whole purpose is to increase your consciousness of God's love, God's beauty, God's laws.*" *Psychic Observer*, Feb. 25th., 1945.

So when the curtain falls, the play and action has ended to the audience present. Yet the actors still exist to appear again in other plays over and over. The curtain falls between actor and audience; yet it rises again and our actors appear to new audiences.

As another writer puts it; "Rebirths are going on all about us and we pay no attention. They are such commonplaces. Mosquitoes from wrigglers, that get their wings atop the water—all kinds of metamorphoses. I don't know why it should surprise me to stick my head up into a new world, and realize that I can draw myself up until I can get entirely into it. It is quite natural."[3]

There are no favorites in the great empire of nature. You live because it is part of the natural law. You return when conditions are right, because it is part of the natural law, and it is open for all to find out for themselves.

---

[3] *Across the Unknown*, White, 50

We do come back,—come back again,—
As long as this big earth rolls.
He Who never wasted a leaf of a tree,
Do you think he could squander souls?

RUDYARD KIPLING

CHAPTER IV

SPIRITUAL CONTACTS

It should be remembered that we are spirits now as much as we ever will be no matter how little of that spirit we manifest through the body of flesh, in our relatively short sojourn on the Earth. Being an individualized Ray of God, the Spiritual Self naturally contains a threefold expression of the Trinity.

The Rays of this threefold cord of expression contact the body through three principal centers:

The Selfconsious, or Rational Ray, contacts the body through the pineal gland. The Spiritual, Intuitional, or life Ray, makes contact through the heart, where the life force enters the blood. The Subconscious, or Instinctive Ray, makes contact through the solar plexus.

These three Rays manifest as three aspects of the One Mind, and these aspects are termed the selfconsious or rational mind, the superconsious or intuitional mind, and the subconscious or instinctive mind.

We use only a small portion of the consciousness we possess,—superconsciousness, self-consciousness or subconsciousness.

No matter what the stress or strain of everyday duties around us, the main object in life is the establishment, growth and expansion of the *Spiritual Self*, for it is this Self that lives on through Eternity. To accomplish this we must keep that Self under the Rays which nourish it; and remember that however exalted and devoted your aims may be, they have no real existence or life until you give them expression by sharing them with others, in thought, word and deed.

PROTECTED DOORS:

The doors of the centers where the Soul contacts the body, are covered with a protective web of etheric matter, which prevents the forces from passing out through them into the higher worlds, until they have been opened normally or abnormally.

When the solar plexus web is opened, the consciousness can pass into the lower astral, leaving the body in a state of astral trance. This is the cause of trance mediumship, for in the absence of the owner's consciousness, other disembodied entities can manifest through the entranced and otherwise empty organism.

But no one need fear such influences, as they can find expression only through those of like negative condition of mind, or those who open their minds or auras to the evil influence of such entities, through giving way to selfish, negative and destructive thoughts and emotions. Therefore, if for no other reason than this, we all should be constantly on our guard against giving way to anger, envy, jealousy or lustful temptations, lest we be swept away into the great currents of such destructive forces in the Astral World as will invade us like whirlwinds and sweep us far beyond anything we had intended or imagined possible.

In other words the so-called psychic senses are not spiritual powers, but the functioning of our five physical senses in the Astral World. Their reports naturally vary with the degree of their training, just as the reports of our physical sight and hearing depend for accuracy upon *their* training.

When the web protecting the brain center is opened, the consciousness is allowed to pass out partially into the higher astral and mental worlds, which produces the condition of clairaudience, clairvoyance or clairsentience.

The ability of the consciousness thus to soar to the higher

worlds, when carried to its highest degree, allows it to ascend above even the mental worlds into the higher Spirit Worlds in a condition of ecstacy or inspirational trance called *Samadhi*; in this condition Divine Spiritual Realities and ultimate God-Consciousness are experienced.

WITHDRAWAL OF RAYS:

In reverse order, at the time of death, the Rays are withdrawn from their respective centers. To this there are exceptions, under which conditions the two Higher Rays are withdrawn without causing the death of the body, as the Life Ray is left still functioning.

When the Life Ray is withdrawn the other two Rays must necessarily cease their activities, as naturally the organism cannot function when the life forces are withdrawn.

According to the degree to which the Selfconscious Ray is withdrawn it leaves the body in a state of semiconsciousness, sleep or trance, with the other two Rays still functioning.

SECOND CHILDHOOD:

These details give us a clew to the phenomenon called "second childhood," for when the object of life has been accomplished, as the Spiritual Self withdraws, it leaves the body still living as before, but under the control only of the sub-conscious mind. This continues to function, largely as a result of habit or routine, dominated by the strongest impressions made on the mind. These are usually impressions of experiences gained in childhood or adolescence. Hence these strongly marked events of childhood are often clearly remembered and referred to as of recent date, while those of later date, which made little distinct impression, are often forgotten. Because these earlier childhood impressions now dominate, and because there is little reasoning power left, the condition is called "second childhood."

HUMAN ANIMALS:

The withdrawal of the Selfconscious Ray leaves behind only a semi-intelligent human-animal, with symptoms of more or less feeble-mindedness. If its training has been constructive and happy, this animal-self will be as easy to care for as any kindly disposed, well trained animal. But if the personality has been untrained, selfish, wilful and inharmonious, when the Spiritual Self has withdrawn its control, there is left behind only a very unruly, irritable, selfish and ill-disposed human-animal to take care of.

Under such conditions this should be recognized, and such a person should not be expected to live up to his former standards of conduct, but should be given the kind thoughtful care that would be given to any aging pet animal. Usually such cases can be better cared for in some well organized home for the aged, where they are often happier and more contented, after the adjustment is made.

SOULLESS HUMANS:

When the Spiritual Ray is withdrawn it naturally leaves behind only a soulless human-animal, without conscience or heart qualities, and with no spiritual overshadowing to control its animal propensities. The object of life having been attained as far as possible in this incarnation, there remains nothing to be desired on earth by the Spiritual Self, so it loses interest in the physical body, and therefore no longer is attracted to it. It then turns its attention inward and withdraws from the physical leaving behind the "soulless human-animal."

Also when the human personality persistently refuses to respond to the influences of the Spiritual Self, and so fails to develop the spiritual qualities of love, compassion and tenderness, it naturally degenerates, for the spiritual cord which attaches it to the Spiritual Self, shrivels and becomes atrophied from lack of use. This ultimately cuts the personality off from its spiritual Source, and leaves it the soulless human animal, although still retaining its mentality, and its degree of intelligence.

There is an important distinction both in quality and degree between this type of soulless human, and that of those experiencing "second childhood." In the first instance, second childhood is due to the conscious withdrawal of the Spiritual Self or Soul, while in the case of the degenerates, it is due, not to a withdrawal of the Soul, but to the degeneration of the tie connecting the personality with the Soul.

This does not constitute a "lost soul" for the soul being immortal, cannot be "lost." It withdraws into the Heaven Worlds, there to remain until it can gather the materials necessary to build up a new human personality in which to reincarnate. What is lost is the personality, since it is cut off from its Spiritual Source.

LOST PERSONALITIES:

These lost personalities may have sufficient spiritual emanations embedded in their finer bodies, and in their "permanent atoms" to cause them to reincarnate one or more times, but each time in a more and more degenerate human form until the stage of imbecility or complete idiocy is reached.

Upon the death of such a one, the atoms of its various bodies disintegrate and return to the elements whence they came. But the *intelligent* soulless beings often degenerate into "Jack-the-Rippers," "Dillengers" and other monsters of crime, who can commit the greatest atrocities without a twinge of conscience, remorse or regret for their crimes. No doubt there are many such soulless beings among the Nazis and Japanese who inflicted such bestial and sadistic tortures on captured prisoners. They are not capable of regret for their crimes, because there is no soul present, with its forces of love and compassion to bring forth such regret.

Upon the death of such soulless degenerates, since death does not change their character, they still retain their evil nature, and bestial desires. They thus have an evil influence on all the mortal minds which are at all affinitized to such tendencies. Thus they become as near as we can conceive of as being discarnate "devils."

PSYCHIC INFLUENCES:

Since at first we carry with us the conditions under which we passed out, until we have been purged from them or outgrown them, ordinarily when we return to our friends on earth, we naturally bring with us those conditions, as we have explained in *Realms of the Living Dead*. It should therefore be understood as a fundamental law of the astral world, that without special training, no person in the astral can come close enough to contact the aura of his friends on earth, without unconsciously and automatically bringing with him and imposing on that party, the physical, astral and mental conditions, from which he suffered or experienced as he left the body at death.

This explains why many sensitive persons soon develop the symptoms of the malady with which a deceased loved one passed out. Such persons suffer just as acutely as though they really had a physical disease, yet a careful physical examination reveals all the vital organs in a normal condition. These cases are often diagnosed as imagination or "neuroses," or even "hysteria" or "insanity" by the family physicians who are not familiar with the results of psychic research, or the laws of occultism. Such patients are simply suffering from *astral conditions*, unwittingly thrown over them by deceased loved ones, who are trying to gain recognition, and the stronger the tie between them, the greater the influence and the greater the reaction. This frequently ceases or is "cured" when the source is recognized. If it is not ended, its effects should be stopped by repeatedly challenging the departed one, and demanding that he withdraw from the aura of the suffering one, and remain outside it in the future; such physical conditions if allowed to continue long, may act reflexly and set up actual diseases in physical form.

METAPHYSICAL MEANS:

These are the stubborn cases which are often "given up by all doctors" yet are frequently cured by Christian Science, New Thought Affirmations, Auto Suggestion, etc. The instruction and personal magnetism of the healer, and the resulting discussions, inform the departed one, more or less, of his responsibility for the conditions, and induce him to withdraw his influence.

One of our students went through an experience of this sort. When her husband passed over, after suffering for a week with very distressing heart conditions, she found herself much distressed with the same symptoms. Believing that the trial of his sudden passing and the strain of subsequent events had brought on heart trouble, she sought medical advice, but after several elaborate tests, no organic heart trouble could be discovered. Finally she called in a young doctor who had had some experience with metaphysics, and in whom she had great faith. He pointed out to her that she had merely taken on the condition which had caused her husband's death, and that the pain and discomfort were psychically imposed. Very soon after this explanation, and by following proper instructions, the trouble ceased entirely.

A SUICIDE CASE:

A few cases from our medical practice will further illustrate this law. One patient complained that she frequently felt a compelling influence to commit suicide, with a razor, when she was in the bathroom. She had spent large sums of money in many months of treatment by psychologists and psychiatrists, who had endeavored to trace events of her earlier life back to childhood in an effort to find some fright, frustration or other emotional cause, which might have produced the suicidal impulse, but without result. Our first question gave us the clue.

When asked whether anyone in her family had ever committed suicide with a razor, she replied that her husband had done so, with the blade of his safety razor, in the bathroom about a year before. When we pointed out to her, and to him, who was there in spirit, that, in his efforts to contact her, he unwittingly threw over her the desperate state of mind which had compelled him to commit the act. We asked him to stand outside her aura in the future, and to try to communicate with her through telepathy only. After this explanation while the patient often sensed his presence, she had no further impulse to suicide.

DRINKING CASE:

While lecturing in Topeka, Kansas, we were consulted by a mother concerning the condition of her son, a young man in the middle twenties. About every three or four months he would have drinking spells, lasting from a day or two to a week or more, until he was completely exhausted. After each spell he would bitterly repent, sign the pledge and vow that he would never touch liquor again, saying that he hated it, and it made him sick, but that he could not resist the impulse to drink. Our psychic investigation revealed the fact that his deceased grandfather, who had been a hard drinking Southern Colonel, was the cause of his condition. He said he was trying to teach the boy to "carry his liquor like a gentleman." The boy, however, was too sensitive to stand the strain. When we explained to the grandfather that his influence was ruining both the boy's health and his character, he promised to stay outside his aura, and not to induce him to drink again. Reports from the mother, a year later, showed that there had been no further drinking sprees. We have cured a number of similar cases of periodic drinking by the same methods.

LONDON CASE:

After one of our lectures in the great Queen's Hall, London, a well-to-do woman came to us for help. She said that she had everything in life that she wanted, wealth, good family, social position, abundance of handsome clothes, motor car, town and country house, etc. Her difficulty was that often when she approached the River Thames, she felt a wild impulse to jump in and drown herself. When asked whether she knew anyone who had thus drowned, in the Thames, she replied that her father had drowned himself there some time before. We explained the situation to her and to her father, who had been attracted to her by our inquiry. He said that he had no idea that he was throwing over her his impulse to drown, when he tried to draw close to her with love and affection, and he promised not to do so again. Some months later she reported that she was *still* completely free of the impulse, and could now visit the Thames with perfect freedom.

War Case:

During World War I, a mother asked us for help about the condition of her daughter, who, she thought, might be losing her mind. The trouble was that the girl suddenly developed a fear of the dark; she was especially too frightened to go to sleep without a light in the room. She had been examined by psychiatrists and psycho-analysts without receiving any relief from her terror, and her mother had turned to us in desperation. Our examination revealed the fact that the girl's fiancé had recently been killed in the war, and it was shortly after that time that her attacks of fear began. When asked to explain exactly what took place, she said that as soon as she turned out the light, and got into bed she felt as though some terrible object was slowly rolling toward her and that if it struck her, she would be blown to bits. Further investigation revealed the fact that, while her fiancé lay wounded in a shell crater, an enemy shell rolled down the slope, and exploded as it struck him, blowing his body to bits. As soon as he recovered from the shock in the astral, he naturally sought out his sweetheart, but strangely enough, not to comfort her, but to urge her to marry his chum whom she knew well, so that he might incarnate through them as their child. Of course he had no idea that he was throwing over her all the tragic incidents of his death. When we explained to both of them that was what he was doing, all terror of the dark disappeared and a few months later the chum and she were married, and within a year a baby boy was born to them.

CHAPTER V

DEATH UNDERSTOOD

To be prepared to understand the cessation of the manifestation of our life on earth, we must have a clear understanding of the universal and inevitable experience commonly called death. This experience is dreaded because the untrained mind fears the unknown and the unfamiliar. Recently, in the light of clearer knowledge and better understanding, through scientific research, this dissolution of the physical that the soul may progress, is believed to be one of the fundamental methods of progress along the Path.

Death, when not due to accident, suicide or war, is the voluntary withdrawal of the Life Ray under the direction of the Spiritual Self. It is simply stepping aside from, or *outside* of, one's house of the body, into the "outdoors" of greater light and freedom. Even if there is sometimes a little confusion and strangeness at the change of abode at first, it need be only temporary and momentary.

DOORS OF EXIT:

There are three doors of exit through which the soul may be released at the time of death, the general tendency of one's life, that on which one has focussed his attention, and the degree of focussing, determining the door of exit.

In the case of animals, children or adults whose attention is largel focussed on the physical,—and this includes the thinking and unintelligent masses,—the door of exit is through the solar plexus.

PLATE I—Departure of the Astral Body at death, through the fontanel. According to the clairvoyant vision of Andrew Jackson Davis.

For the mass of kindly disposed and unselfish people,—among whom we find the well meaning good citizens, the compassionate, philanthropic workers for the good of others, – for all these folks whose heart qualities predominate, the exit is made through the door in the region of the heart.

In the case of the mental types, and the more spiritually evolved types, the exit is made, more or less consciously through the fontanels at the top of the head.

Some occult teachers advocate, not merely *drifting to sleep* but practicing consciously withdrawing through the top of the head, for this will facilitate the conscious withdrawing at death. When this ability has been developed, we will be able to withdraw, at death, in full consciousness.

"Stepping outside one's self actually means the practice of making one's own, in imagination, the conditions of the hour of death. . . . Supposing the day came for the Great Adventure of departing hence. . . . One is apt to take this tremendous step quite suddenly. What is it going to be like? Why turn our imagination away from it. . . . Why not entertain ourselves with the buoyancy of anticipation?"[1]

Some teachers claim that as the soul approaches the withdrawal of life and consciousness, it has a preview of the time and place of death, and so is prepared for it and able to predict it.

It is said that a dim orange light in the room during the passing, facilitates the desirable withdrawing through the top of the head.

Apparently this method of exit was known to the priesthood of many lands, down through the ages. From the earliest times the Hindoos pictured man with the cap of an inverted lotus blossom of a thousand petals, with the stalk extending from the top of the head up into the higher worlds.

This illustrates how the Spiritual Self sends down its Rays of personality, and enters the body through the top of the

---

[1] *Across the Unknown*, White, 64.

head. There it blossoms for a few short years, and then returns to its heavenly home over the same route.

Archeologists exploring in the Mimbres Valley in New Mexico in 1929, found over four hundred mummies of primitive Indians, estimated to be at least 1400 years old. The head of each was covered with an earthen bowl, which had a small hole drilled into the bottom, so it would come directly over the top of the head. Through this hole the spirit of the departed was supposed to ascend into the Heaven World.

The almost universal recognition of this method of exit, down through the ages, in widely separated parts of the earth is good evidence that it is a fact in Nature which is commonly recognized.

These details explain why there are conflicts in the reports of observers as to through which door the exit is made. All three types of observers may be correct, as they have been reporting exits through the different centers.

THE PASSING:

From many authentic sources comes the blessed word that the actual passing over, the moment of transition, can be a delightful, easy and happy experience. We quote from some eminent writers, who feel that from all the descriptions given by authorities who are in position to know, whereof they speak, death is a beautiful thing over which there should be no grief, no bitterness, to mar the experience of the one who is passing. Only friends should be around who understand, and who are calm and loving.

"Spirit friends have already come to attend this higher birth. Often they bring garments white and glistening."[2]

When the eminent William Hunter lay dying he is quoted as saying. "If I had strength enough to hold a pen, I would write how easy and delightful it is to die."[3]

---

[2] *Immortality*, Peebles, 36, 38, 39, 44.
[3] *Ibid.*

A Universalist minister, the Rev. J. W. Bailey, the day before he passed over, began to sing, and would sing for hours, saying that it did not tire him to sing, and that he was so happy that he could not help it. . . . He turned his eyes upward and oh, how glorious they looked! They seemed illumined with heavenly light. He opened his eyes and smiling upon his wife said. "I have seen over the river. . . . it is beautiful on this side, but oh, glorious, glorious on the other!". . . . he then said, "Do not grieve," waved his hand and passed on.[4]

When Mrs. Pinkerton, a medium of same note, and a spiritualist lecturer, was passing into death, she exclaimed, "This is a glorious doctrine to die by friends. . . . This is the best day of my life; I hear the angels singing; I am happy, happy, happy!. . . . Doubt no more—I know there is a blessed, glorious, eternal life. . . . The voyage is pleasant."[5]

And from the spirit world we have the following messages! "Now I am quite successfully dead. It wasn't much of an operation after all! It was a pleasurable releasing, quite different from the death-agony idea. . . . That should be looked upon as merely the birth pangs of the spiritual body."[6]

"I feel like a tramp stealing a ride under a car, and sudenly asked into a pullman. Wonderful to be a part, even a little part of anything that moves on with such majesty, beauty and power."[7]

"There is no bump or jar. We keep right on just as we have been going. . . . You shut up your old house and move into a new habitation. . . . There is no sudden jump, which will transfer you. *You take over what you are*."[8]

The following is a vivid description of a passing over:

---

[4] *Ibid.*
[5] *Ibid.*
[6] *Across the Unknown*, White.
[7] *Ibid.*
[8] *Ibid.*

"I discovered by certain whispers which it was supposed I was unable to hear, and from certain glances of
commiseration, which it was supposed I was unable to
see, that I was near death. . . . Presently my mind began to
dwell, not only on the happiness which was to come, but
on that which I was actually enjoying. I saw long forgotten
forms, playmates, companions of my youth, and of my old
age, who one and all smiled upon me. They did not smile
with any compassion;—that I felt I no longer needed—but
with that sort of kindness which is exchanged by people
who are equally happy. I saw my mother, father, and sisters. . . . They did not speak yet they communicated to me
their unaltered and unalterable affection. At about the same
time when they appeared, I made an effort to realize my
bodily situation. . . . that is I endeavored to connect my
soul with my body, which lay on the bed in my house. . . .
the endeavor failed. . . . I was dead."[9]

CONDUCT OF FRIENDS:

As we have stated elsewhere, and we would like to be
emphatic about it; we should say farewell to our loved
ones with no more grief than would be natural if they were
starting on a long journey, to another country, and were
intending to stay for a long time. We shall see them again,
and will be in communication with them if we desire. . . .
Instead of spending time and force in useless grief and
mourning, the time should be *spent in quiet meditation*,
and in an effort to correlate our consciousness with theirs
and assure them of our love and understanding. Mourning
clothes should not be worn, nor should constant visits be
paid to the grave, for all such acts and thoughts *tend to hold
the departed one down to the discarded body*, through the
law of attraction.

The recently deceased is often strongly attached to the
discarded physical body, and for some time hence, haunts

---

[9] *One Hundred Cases of Survival after Death*, Baird.

its burial place. But it is thus held only as a result of thought or desire, the desire to see what becomes of the former outer garment it wore while on earth. Therefore, cremation is always desirable. . . . because it consumes the physical magnetism, and this releases the desceased at once from that source of attraction to the Physical World. Great care should be taken to see that either burial or cremation is not carried out, until the astral body has had time to withdraw completely from the physical body, or considerable suffering may result. . . . The attending physician should not sign the death certificate, nor the undertaker be called, until there is absolute surety that the soul has really left the body.[10]

Peace and quiet should prevail in the death chamber, and there should be no hysterical beseeching of the loved one to return. This often brings him back for a few minutes, only to have to go through the process of dying all over again.

Seen and understood in the light of present inspiration and spiritual revelations, *there is no death, no real death.* There is only transition, a changing of form and state; only the renunciation of the physical body for a lighter, freer and less unwieldy one. It is the dissolution of time and space. It is living in another atmosphere with our own selfsame consciousness as we had while on the earth plane, but with a clearer vision and a wider understanding. It holds no terrors for those who will learn.

So, death should be a quiet loosening of the magnetic bonds which hold us to the body, and a letting-go of the strong earth desires for a further life on Earth; the more one clings to Earth, the greater the futile struggle against the inevitable transition.

And so, as one writer puts it. "Death, which is only the shedding of the outer envelope, in no way affects the immortal man. It is not a sponge which cleans the slate in a moment; not a sieve that, while separating the chaff from

---

[10] *For further details, see Realms of the Living Dead*, Curtiss, 65-66.

the wheat, purifies the soul; not a moral chemist, that so manipulates character as perfect in the twinkling of an eye. And yet death, or conditions to which death introduces the individual, offers better and higher facilities for perpetual progress."[11]

---

[11] *Immortality,* Peebles, 55.

Chapter VI

EFFECTS OF PRAYER

Prayer is defined as "The mode of addressing a divine or sacred power, in which there predominates the mood and intent of reverent entreaty. In this sense it is a characteristic feature of the higher religions, and we might even say that Christianity, or Mohammedanism, ritually viewed, is in its utmost essence, a service of prayer."[1]

As we have pointed out elsewhere, the object of all religions is the worship of the Divine; and the primary object of all worship is personal contact with, and realization of the Divine. But as there is a method of mechanism by which the whole manifested universe comes into physical expression, so is there a method, or mechanism, by which conscious contact is made between the human personality and those higher expressions of God, toward which the heart aspires.

While there are many avenues by which this contact is made, ranging from contemplation, meditation, and silent aspiration, to the sudden despairing cry for help and protection in times of crises, nevertheless the avenue most readily available to the average consciousness, is prayer, as commonly understood. This does not mean that one must necessarily repeat certain stipulated words as set forth by another, for each heart can usually formulate its own words, to express its own desires and needs. But, as words both symbolize and embody definite ideas, when properly voiced they can be used to produce specific effects.

---

[1] *Encyclopedia Britannica*, 11th. Edition, Vol. 22, 256-b.

EFFECTIVE PRAYERS:

Effective prayers are not mere combinations of words, carefully thought out by the intellect, and arranged as a literary composition. Such prayers rise scarcely above the ceiling of the room in which they are uttered. To be effective they must spring forth spontaneously, and express the feelings and aspirations of the heart. The degree of their spirituality determines the height to which they will rise in the heavenly realms.

St. James emphasizes the need that the prayer be a fervent one when he truly said: "The effective, fervent prayer of a righteous man available much in its working."[2]

Neither is prayer merely a supplication, a sending up of a plea or a wish for somethin we desire to obtain. Constructive prayer is creative, and in order that it may be effective, it must be approached with a greath warmth of desire; a realization of something lacking in our spiritual life and attainment. Prayer enlarges our consciousness of the reality of Truth for our own personal use, and our realization of our oneness with the Great Source must be expanded, and go up to meet the fulfillment of our prayer. Our capacity to receive the answer must be great enough to allow it to come to us. In other words, we pray to be made great enough to receive and be worthy of that for which we ask.

Reports from authorities in the spirit world confirm our statement that the mere repetition of words has little effect on the powers evoked. Repeating prayers by rote has little more effect than repeating the multiplication table.

Prayer, then, is a constant projection of your spiritual being, heart and soul; a constant realization of your Spiritual Self.

One great writer tells us about prayer as he received the message from spirit teachers:

"You must know that there are appointed guardians of prayer here whose duty it is to analyse and sift prayers offered and sent up by those on earth, and separate them into

---

[2] *St. James*, 5, 16.

divisions and departments; to pass them on to be examined by others and dealt with according to their merits and powers. . . .

"In order that this may be done perfectly, it is necessary that we study the vibrations of prayer, as your scientists study the vibrations of light and sound, and as they are able to analyze and classify and separate the rays of light, so are we able to deal with your prayers. And as there are light rays with which they are confessedly unable to deal, so many prayers present to us those deeper tones which are beyond the range of our knowledge. These we pass on to those of higher grades, to be dealt with in their greater wisdom. And do not think that these prayers are always found among the prayers of the wise. They are frequently found in the prayers of children, whose petitions and sighs are as carefully considered here as the prayers of nations. . . . And what applies to prayer, also may be applied to the exercise of the will in directions not so legitimate. Hate and impurity and greed, and other sins of the spirit and mind, take on here a solidity which is not seen or realized in your sphere: and these also are dealt with according to their merits. . . . And. . . . alas, those who say that the angels cannot grieve, know little of our love for our brethren still battling on earth. Could they see us dealing with some of these misusings of the Father's great gift, they would probably love us more and exalt us less."[3]

The answer to the prayer is not given fully and effectively when the prayer is not directed in the right direction, for the projection of the will must be straight at the end desired, or the effect is weakened. When the prayer is weakened — without faith — or is actuated by unworthy motives, it does not link up or harmonize with the wills of those whose duty it is to take care of prayers, and the end is not attained.

"We in spirit life pray for help whenever we want it, let the object be what it may; but not if it is an evil object.

---

[3] *Lowlands of Heaven*, Owen, 138-39-40.

In the latter case prayer certainly is undesirable, for it is the cause of attracting to you spirits which will aid you in accomplishing your purpose perhaps, but they will only increase your unhappiness afterwards; if you have strong willpower you are tempting *them*. On the other hand if you pray for a good object, you benefit the spirits whom you draw around you. It is good for them to help others, and in helping you they help themselves. Thus you see prayer is a spiritual force which you can put into operation if you have will-power enough.

"Prayer is, therefore, not merely aspiration, it is something like advertising your wants. . . . You should, of course, pray to God rather than to the spirits directly. He permits spirits to execute His decrees. . . . We all live under His laws, and nothing can happen *contrary* to His laws. Whatever is done must be done by Divine sanction, and to Him our prayers should be addressed. By *longing* we do not mean *praying*. Prayer is a more active form of longing. . . . Prayer asks, and love grants.[4]

"We are continually broadcasting our most secret thoughts and desires. We are accountable for what we send out; our desire does not die in our breasts, but it goes out as something we have launched, to run straight ahead on its appointed course, until the force of its projection is exhausted, or until it meets a more powerful or deflecting force. . . . That is part of our responsibility: to send out as far as human frailty will permit, only wholesome impetus into the intricate cross currents of world life."[5]

"The formulation of a need into a thought, a petition, with the sure *submerging of self*, that comes with prayer to what is greater and higher than self, is a beneficent operation to the individual, and is a definite projection unto the unobstructed universe.

"It is a very good thing to teach children to pray. Prayer

---

[4] *Immortality*, Peebles, 253-4.
[5] *The Betty Book*, White, 134.

is an actuality and gives them a belief. The world has got along very well on a belief in prayer, for the voicing of a desire or an emotion makes it concrete. It clears it in your own mind, if nothing else. And maybe when you have formulated it, you find you do not want it; or if you do. . . . 'God helps those who help themselves.'"[6]

"Prayer is the projection of your spiritual being, heart and soul. It is the conscious assembling of your highest self. "Constructive prayer consists in the realization of, not spiritual needs but spiritual lacks."[7]

Raising our consciousness and realization of our oneness with the Great Creator, or Power, is the channel through which our prayers are answered. Our *thoughts* and *words* go up as prayers, and not one but is answered for us or against us. Power is given to us by the Spirit to change our thoughts from those of negation to those of Heaven. Words and thoughts of Love, Joy, Peace, uplifting and constructive thoughts and words, have power and potency. They represent Divine Power and Reality. Their opposites are merely an inversion of them, and therefore have no power of their own. These words of Love, Peace, Order, Harmony, Beauty and Perfection, are words that carry with them tremendous power to bring these attributes into our bodies, our lives and our affairs. If we think such thoughts and speak such words, aloud or inwardly to our Soul, we became filled with the Light and Power of Heaven.

Prayer can attune you with spirit forces, but it takes something else too. Real prayer is thought, word, high motive, endeavor.

> "More things are wrought by prayer
> Than this world dreams of. Wherefore let thy voice,
> Rise like a fountain for me night and day.
> For what are men better than sheep or goats
> That nourish a blind life within the brain,

---

[6] *Unobstructed Universe*, White, 253.
[7] *The Betty Book*, White, 135-36.

If, knowing God, they lift not hands of prayer
Both for themselves and those who call them
friend?"[8]

PRAYER IN ACTION:

Every sincere prayer, every spiritual aspiration, every constructive thought or emotion, every unselfish deed, engenders a constructive vibration which ascends from the physical to that higher realm with which it affinitizes. There it is immediately noted by the spiritual workers in that realm, who do all they can to manifest the desired result or answer, to the Soul who sent forth the vibration. This of course is more or less subject to the consiousness and karma of that individual Soul. Such constructive aspirations and vibrations pierce the clouds of mentality and miasma overhanging humanity, like skyrockets illuminating the night. And, most important of all, they leave a trail of spiritual fire behind them, which becomes a channel of light, through which the return currents from the unseen worlds, can penetrate the overshadowing, miasmic fog, and reach humanity. In other words, such vibrations make rifts in the dark douds, through which beams of light from the Spiritual Sun can shine down upon mankind.

SPIRITUAL FORCES:

Thus, amid the most terrible conditions of inharmony, crime and war, there are also manifesting tremendous forces of Spiritual Light, uplift, and encouragement, for there are vast and highly organized groups of advanced Souls in most of the unseen realms, who have dedicated their lives to the service of humanity, under the direction of the Christ. These are ever seeking avenues of contact with mankind, even more eagerly and persistently than are the evil forces, that through such avenues they may pour their powers of love, inspiration and constructive power, and enlightenment for the help, guidance and comfort of humanity, during these

---

[8] *Morte d'Arthur*, Tennyson, L. 247.

"days of tribulation." All such who have enlisted in the service of the Christ, together with the more advanced Beings, who stand close around the throne of God, have long watched and waited for this time to come. They know well that, only as they can build a bridge of love, understanding and service between themselves and humanity, and inspire mankind to live a truly and earnestly helpful spiritual life, can both they and humanity hope to accomplish the work of the Lord Christ, and thus shorten these "days of tribulation."

SPIRITUAL HELPERS:

These multitudes of advanced Souls in the Higher Realms of the unseen worlds, who have enlisted in the army of the Lord, and unselfishly seek to help humanity, together with the angelic hosts that surround the Christ as a great body guard of Cosmic Force, as He prepares to descend into manifestation on Earth, have more than once begged the Father for more time during which humanity may repent and be redeemed.

So the great day of adjustment has been pushed back, and pushed back, time and time again. But alas, cosmic forces can be influenced or diverted only temporarily, as they move inevitably forward to their destined manifestation, unless they are neutralized by opposite vibrations of greater power.

While there are many periods when similar astronomical, astrological and astral influences have prevailed, yet, just as one day differs from another that is seemingly identical, so is it with the greater cycle of the ages. The night is now far spent and dawn draweth nigh. The New Day is at hand, the Day of change, the Day of tribulation, "which has not been since the beginning of time, no nor ever shall be." It is the day of seeming disaster, but is in reality the Day of Cleansing and Purifying.[9]

This general belief verified through the ages by experience, is explicitly explained by our Cosmic Soul Science, which

---

[9] For further details see *World Conditions*, Curtiss.

holds, that, "every sound in the visible world awakens its corresponding sound in the invisible realms, and arouses to action some force or other on the occult side of Nature. . . . All these find an echo. . . . even on the terrestrial plane, in the lives that swarm in the terrene atmosphere, *thus prompting them to action*."[10]

PRAYER SERVICE:

The *Universal Religious Fellowship* has a daily prayer service, at which time the names of all those desiring special help, especially for their health, or while undergoing an operation, are relayed to the Invisible Helpers.

When the author's mother was asked how such cases were handled in the invisible, her reply was:

"The Christ force would find its way to the students requiring help, even without the names being given. The condition of those needing help calls for it, as we might say, automatically. The entire class is looked over and the bare spots discerned." She also said that when prayers are said for her they invoke forces of inspiring, joyous, spiritual forces from the higher realms, all of which help her to progress.

That such attention to the needs of our students produces beneficial results is evidenced by the fact that, for more than thirty years, when students' need for help during operations is mentioned no operation has been unsuccessful, and no post operative infection or hemorrhage has developed. Often such cases are the "miracle cases" because they usually recover so rapidly that they are out of the hospital in half the usual time.

"Man offers himself to God. He stands before Him as the canvas before the painter, or the marble before the sculptor. At the same time *he asks for His grace*, exposes his needs and those of his brothers in suffering. The modest, the ignorant, the poor are more capable of this self-denial,

_____
[10] *The Secret Doctrine*, Blavatsky, 111, 451.

than the rich and the intellectual. When it possesses such characteristics, prayer may set in motion a strange phenomenon, *the miracle.*"[11]

SPIRITUAL PRAYERS:

Spiritually inspired prayers are practically dictated by high spiritual Beings in the Higher Realms. They are not mere pleasant-sounding pious words, strung together for their literary effect, but are practically *mantrams*, whose repetition invokes forces from particular Hierarchies to produce special effects. The following examples[12] given the author will illustrate our meaning. They also embody the teachings we have given in the previous chapters:

INVOCATION TO THE DIVINE INDWELLER:

Come forth, O Lord of Life and Love and Beauty!
Thou Who art my Higher Self, and yet art God!
And manifest through this body of Thine,
That it may outpicture Thy radiant perfection.
All that Thou art within.
Even so, manifest through me, O Lord. Amen.

INVOCATION TO THE I AM PRESENCE:

O Eternal Being, Thou loving I Am Presence
Whose I am, and Whom I serve;
Thou art in me and I in Thee;
Thou art mine and I am Thine.
Thou art my eternal Pattern;
Make me more and more like Thee. Amen.

HEALING INVOCATION:

O Thou loving and helpful Master Jesus!
Thou Who gavest to Thy disciples power to heal the
  sick!
We, recognizing Thee and realizing Thy Divine
  Presence with us,

---

[11] *Man, the Unknown*, Carrel. 148.
[12] These and other similar prayers, for almost every occasion will be found in *Dynamic Prayers*, Curtiss.

Ask Thee to lay Thy Hands upon us in healing love.
Cleanse us from all our sins, and by the Divine Power
  of Omnipotent Life
Drive out the atoms of inharmony and disease,
And fill our bodies full to overflowing, with
Life, and Love and Immunity.

PROTECTING INVOCATION:

O Christ! surround and fill me and (Here mention the
  person, room, home, or other object you wish to have
  protected.)
With the seven-fold flame of Divine Love and
  Wisdom,
That it may purify, illumine and guide me in all things.
May its Spiritual Fire form a rampart of Living Flame,
Around me and (The ones or things mentioned above.)
To protect us from all harm.
May it radiate to every heart, consuming all evil.
And intensifying all good.
In the Name of the Living Christ we ask it.

CHAPTER VII

PRAYERS FOR THE DEAD

We repeat here for emphasis, what we have said on this subject in *Realms of the Living Dead*, page 49: "Prayers for the loved ones who have gone over surround them with comforting, helpful and protective thought forces, and they also serve to call the invisible helpers to their needs."

As prayer can thus reach the higher realms, and bring to mankind, the help of those over there, just so, on the other hand, can prayers, especially for our loved ones, reach them and have their specific effects. This two-way process is the basis of offering prayers for the dead.

Testimony from the spirit world says; "For those who have gone on into the perfect understanding, it is ever good to pray. Why? Because the Universe is one. You pray for us, we pray for you. You can be in a sense our guardian angels, as we are yours."[1]

From the most ancient times, prayers for the dead have been recognized as being beneficial to the departed souls. Wherever there is a belief in the continued existence of the personality of man through and after death, religion naturally concerns itself with the relations between the living and the dead.

ANCESTOR WORSHIP:

Prayers for the dead bring to mind the ancestor worship among the Chinese and Japanese, and other Oriental peoples,

---

[1] *Unobstructed Universe*, White, 240.

wherein direct communication with the departed is recognized as being made. They are thus kept informed of all the major events in the life of the family, and their aid is sought through prayer to them.

Not only is this belief held by the Orientals, from the earliest ages, but it is also found in nearly all other religions which assume, not only that the soul is immortal, and thus survives death, but that personal communication is possible. This doctrine was held by the early church fathers, varying in degree from St. Augustine's prayer for the rest of his mother's soul, to the extreme statement of Tertullian, that, "the widow who does not pray for her dead husband, has as good as divorced him."

EGYPTIAN BELIEFS:

The doctrine of immortality and everlasting life, and the belief in the resurrection of a spiritual body, are the brightest and most prominent features of the ancient Egyptian religion. The many religious texts found appealed mightily to all, from the highest to the lowest, for they were believed to give man power in the world beyond the grave, and to enable him to gain everlasting life.

FORMULA OF EGYPTIAN PRAYERS:

Petitions were addressed to the God, or Gods, of the community on behalf of the dead, and they contained petitions for the welfare of the departed in the world beyond the grave.

Their realization as to the reality of a future existence was very definite and they believed that the life hereafter was similar to that which thy had led upon earth.

The most important collection of these prayers and rituals is found in Professor Budge's *The Book of the Dead*. They can scarcely be called inspiring because they are nearly all concerned with the allaying of the fears of the departed, and protecting them from the fears of the astral world.

CATHOLIC DOCTRINE:

According to the Catholic doctrine, as stated in the authoritative *Catholic Dictionary*; "Prayers for the dead benefit the souls in Purgatory. . . . The souls in Purgatory are aided by the suffrages of the faithful. . . . They are benefitted by the mass, indulgences and good works, such as prayers, fasting, alms, etc. . . . The satisfactory indulgence of good works, which consists of the remission of punishment due to sin, is transferred to the poor souls. . . . It is reasonable to hold that God always applies the satisfactory merits of good works, offered for the dead, to the poor souls; to those souls for whom they are offered. It is held that the pains of Purgatory are measured by years and days, and that each forgiven soul was supposed to have to endure an amount of suffering in proportion to the guilt of its sins, and the prayers and penance of the living availed to shorten this penance time in Purgatory."[2]

It is therefore possible that the masses sincerely said, in addition to the upward striving of the *soul* itself, may be said, "to pray itself out of Purgatory," in due time.

In liturgies of various churches, were lists of the names of the dead, to be commemorated at the Eucharist, from the days of St. Paul, who prayed for the rest of the Soul of Onesiphorous (2nd. Timothy, 1-16.) to the present day.

MORMON DOCTRINE:

"The mormon Temples are not 'churches.' They are religious centers, for sacred ordinances—ritualistic courses of work and study—done by living Mormons for the benefit of deceased relatives and friends. Through these ordinances those in the spirit world are brought nearer to Divine Perfection,—prepared for eternity."[3]

---

[2] *New Catholic Dictionary*, 781.
[3] *Pathfinder*, Nov, 1945.

ANGLICANS DISAGREE:

"The Church of England believed at one time that the prayers for the dead were of no avail, since, according to their 'Church Association,' the *believer* inherits everlasting life, and needs no such prayers, whilst the *unbeliever's* lot is everlasting condemnation. . . . a destiny which no prayers after death can alter. However the 'Church Times' apparently does not agree, probably in the light of modern research and enlightenment. In one of its recent issues, it printed an article containing the words; 'God. . . . must surely design that our life after death shall be in a state in which our spirits can mature. . . . the life which the departed live is a state of purification and of progress. . . . .'

"Reflections such as these constrain us to appreciate the naturalness of remembering the departed in our prayers."[4]

PURGATORY:

According to the Roman Catholic Faith, Purgatory is a state of suffering after death, in which the souls of those who die in venial sin, and those who still owe some debt of temporal punishment for mortal sin, are rendered fit to enter heaven.[5]

Since the mere incident of leaving the physical plane does not change the character of the personality of a man, he carries with him the quality of the vibrations of his mind and desires, and he is thus surrounded by the conditions which he generated on earth. If these were of the "earth earthy," they naturally hold the person in close mental and magnetic touch with the earth.

These material vibrations naturally weigh him down with their materiality, and prevent him from rising to the Higher Realms above. He therefore remains earthbound, until those lower vibrations have been eliminated, by the process of transmutation and spiritualization. This process is called

---

[4] *Psychic News*, Oct. 4th, 1945.
[5] *Encyclopedia Britannica*, 11th. Edition, Vol. 22, 262 B.

purgation, and the state in which it takes place is called Purgatory.

This process of redemption is a very real condition, and may last for years, according to the efforts made by the Soul to reach higher levels.

Since we have described the low conditions of purgatory in some detail, in *Realms of the Living Dead*, we will refer to them here only as follows: "I have seen in the lower spheres of darkness, clusters of societies and cities of moral degradation, in the streets of which, undeveloped spirits were engaged in disputations, quarrels, enmities and pitiful ravings. They delighted to annoy and torture each other—delighted to live in a measure, their earthy lives over again, and to influence gamblers in their dens, inebriates in their wretched retreats, and debauchees in their haunts of crime. These scenes make angles weep, and I mention them with sadness. And yet the same God is over all, the same influx of life sustains all, and there is hope for all in the future."[6]

"There is a very definite reality in 'hell' and 'purgatory,' not precisely as the theologians have it perhaps, but a reality. But no one comes to the perfect understanding without the necessity of a time of readjustment, and of wishing he had done differently."[7]

And again, the same spiritual teacher has said; "Take the person who has fostered or allowed in himself a gradual growth or accumulation of petty griefs, envies, angers, unkindly judgments, and intolerances toward his associates, amounting finally to a complex that actually makes a character. . . . These are the 'negatives' that must be eradicated in 'purgatory,' if you want to call it that. Such a person must come to a complete understanding, complete selflessness, complete love. And *by his own effort*.

"It is only the emotional things that really count. If people are big enough to live right emotionally, the concrete thing

---

[6] *Immortality*, Peebles, 91.
[7] *The Unobstructed Universe*, White, 240.

can be over-ridden. Because—and I want you all to get this—*because, nothing that happens to an individual is as important as what that individual thinks about it.*"[8]

This process of purgation may not invoke suffering, unless the negative conditions generated are mostly sinful and grossly material. Otherwise it may be just a period through which the Soul passes while having its attention turned from things of the material life, to those of the spiritual life. For instance, the loved ones often spend years in intimate contact with the lives and affairs of those left behind, as long as they are greatly concerned about them. With such concern prominently occupying their minds, they pay little attention to their progress and purgation. It is these whom our *prayers* especially help, since they turn the attention of such, to higher things. Therefore do not think of the process, of purgation as necessarily one of intense suffering, unless the departed cling desperately to the old ideas, habits, and desires of the earth life. If they have lived a good temperate life, they may enjoy a happy existence "over there" for many years, surrounded by their relatives and friends.

HELL FIRE:

Modern research has abundantly shown that, while the *Christian Bible* may not be historically accurate, the allegories and parables, are *universally true* and are grouped and arranged to illustrate symbolically some feature of the growth of the Soul. They serve to illustrate phases of experience, through which every soul passes during its journey toward conscious union with the Divine.

This arouses great controversy and there is no doctrine that has aroused so much debate as that of "hell-fire." When this is mentioned in the Bible it refers to the process of transmutation, in which evil is transmuted into good. The fires are the fires of purification and transmutation, which consume all that is false or impure. These fires are those of

---

[8] *The Unobstructed Universe*, White, 245.

karma that the personality has lighted, and in which it must stand until all is converted into *good*. The soul will not be left in hell, but will gather to itself the experiences necessary to clothe itself in immortality. Hell endures *forever and ever* simply because there is no end to eternity, or evolution, and there will always be some dross to burn out and be purified and transmuted.

Hell is separation from God, and the greater the separation, the greater the suffering.[9]

But let us repeat again for emphasis: While we all have to pass through the stage of purgation, necessary for our advance into higher realms, we do not all have to pass through a "*Purgatory*" of intense suffering, or through the fires of "Hell." Only the extremely wicked and unrepentant, whose vibrations automatically affinitize them with those conditions, must do so.

"Thou wilt not leave my soul in hell (to Sheol)—, neither wilt thou suffer Thine Holy One to see corruption." (Psalms, 16, 10.)

And so, as we have said elsewhere, when we pass to another plane, we are surrounded and conditioned by the thought forms we have accumulated on the earth plane.

Those who have believed in, and thought much about hell fire after death, especially those who have greatly feared it, often suffer much from such thought-forms of fire. We were once present at a materializing séance, in which a form materialized, completely surrounded by such thought-forms of fire, which were so dense as to actually bring heat into the room. He was writhing in pain, as if from an actual cloud of flame. He appealed piteously for help. When we explained that he was suffering only from his own thought creation, magnified by fear and that he could be released by calling on the Christ for help, he prayed fervently and a Ray of cool white light shot down and dissipated the cloud of fire.

It is no wonder then that this stage of transition toward

---

[9] For further details see chapter on *Hell Fire*, Voice of Isis, Curtiss, 78.

the Higher Realms is recognized by almost all religions. This is most eloquently expressed in Dante's immortal *"The Inferno,"* and Milton's *"Paradise Lost"* although both of these great works stress largely the lowest depths of such conditions, in the slums of the astral.

PRAYER FOR THE DEAD:

O Thou Great Almighty One! from whose heart all mankind has sprung! We pray that Thou wilt focus the Rays of Thy Love, Light and Life, upon those loved ones of ours, who have graduated from this school of earth life, into Thy higher school of the Soul.

Send to them, we pray, the hosts of Thy angelic workers, that they may welcome, guide, and teach our loved ones the ways of the higher life.

Teach them how to live in ever greater consciousness of Thine all-encompassing love.

Teach them how to realize, imbibe and assimilate Thy Power, that they may transmute, and be purged from, all Earth conditions that hold them back from their continued progress, into ever higher realms of Thy spirit-world.

Banish all fear and sorrow, with the joy of a new and more Spiritual life.

Teach them how to purge themselves of all that might affinitize them to those unhappy souls, who are still in the regions of darkness, either on earth or in the after-life, who would seek to drag them down to that level.

Teach them to right the wrongs they have done on earth, as much as possible.

Teach them how to comfort and inspire those they have left behind, that they too, may seek to press ever forward in the Spiritual life, under Thy guidance.

Thus may all in the two worlds be drawn closer to one another, and to Thee, in the oneness of Thy divine Light, Life and Love.

CHAPTER VIII

GRADUATION

Earth may be considered as the seminary of heaven, where the Soul is placed to contact the material, that it may develop and perfect a more mature individuality. It is the rudimentary school, where the most material conditions for spiritual development, may be contacted and mastered.

A SOUL SCHOOL:

Earth conditions therefore, constitute a common or grade school for the Soul. Their lessons prepare us for greater Soul growth and unfoldment, as we learn to express more and more of the spiritual qualities of our Real Self under the handicaps of material limitations.

Just as in the common school there are many grades and many teachers, so in the common school of earth-life there are many grades and conditions and many kinds of teachers. The grade, or type of environment in which we start this life, depends on the degree of unfoldment we have obtained in past lives, as we have already explained in a previous chapter. For we bring into this incarnation, the net results of the lessons we have learned in previous lives.

This stock of lessons learned and the character gained, we build into the new personality as inherent abilities, talents, likes and dislikes, the expression of which cannot be accounted for by the Law of Physical Heredity. That Law applies only to the type of body our parents furnish us as an instrument through which to manifest.

WE PROGRESS:

As we make the best use of these inborn qualities, to learn the new lessons which we incarnated to learn, we progress from grade to grade. But if we fail to learn the lessons of life which result in spiritual advancement, we waste our opportunities, and so have to experience the same conditions again and again, in this and even in subsequent incarnations, until the needed qualities have been built into and manifested in our character. So it is of no use for us to try to "play hooky" in this school of life by refusing to face and conquer the conditions which life brings to us, and to learn the lessons contained therein.[1]

We must accept the moral responsibility of the individual, and that he makes his own happiness or unhappiness as he obeys or disobeys Nature's physical and spiritual Laws. And remember that the door to reformation is never closed to any human Soul, here or hereafter.

From the spirit world comes this message: "Each individual comes into the world to do a job, and he comes *here* best and happiest only when it is completed; after he has gathered to himself as nearly as possible his requisite of work and experience. The purpose of the present divulgence is to restore in earth consciousness the necessity of individual effort, and the assurance that the effort will not be wasted. The only assurance of this is a return to the belief in immortality."[2]

The best proof of growth in character is the manifestation of the "fruits of the Spirit," listed by St Paul (Gal. 5, 22.) as, "love, joy, peace, long-suffering, gentleness, kindness, goodness, and faithfulness." When we return to our spiritual home, these are the only things that go with us, for we can take none of this world's goods. We can take only the character we have developed, and a memory of our earthly experiences, together with the satisfaction of a work well done, and the happiness of remembering the little kindnesses,

---

[1] For full details see *Why Are We Here*, Curtiss.
[2] *Unobstructed Universe*, White, 66.

the good deeds, the helpfulness and encouragement we have given, to our fellow travellers on the way. We may also carry over poignant regrets for the many opportunities for advancement we have missed, or neglected, and for a life misspent or wasted; or perhaps we will have remorse for our evil deeds, and the injustices and suffering we have inflicted on others.

WE CONTINUE TO GROW:

We repeat for emphasis what we have said in another chapter, that when we leave this earth plane, we do not immediately reach maturity, nor are we through with lessons. As we are told from the other side:

"Get over any idea that death is going to instantaneously transform you into Celestial Beings. You did not leap into maturity when you graduated from high school into college. There is no sudden jump which will transform you. *You take over what you are.* That is the real continuity. It is not the real continuity of going over to something easier and adapted to all your peculiarities. It is a smooth transition. . . . You've got to do away with that superstition that your handicaps here will be instantly eliminated there. Get adapted here and then you will enter without conditions. It is a smooth, beautiful thing, this continuity. The division between the lines is an imaginary equator. . . . What you are doing now carries over. . . . Your real wealth and capital, which will rehabilitate you in *any* change that comes to you, is the extent to which you have developed this *Inner Reality*. It is what gives strength to character, the power to convince and influence others, the calm acceptance of temporary destructions of one's impermanent possessions and surroundings."[3]

And as another communicator expresses it: "There is no deception possible about the status of those who pass out of the body. It is not possible — permanently — for a man to disguise himself, and by the assumption of titles or styles to

---

[3] *Across the Unknown*, White, 108-09-10.

pass himself as something he is not. Not all the uniforms, not all the bestowed decorations, not all the orders or honorifics, of men, will change a mean spirited man or woman into a noble soul. Time spent in the service of humanity, will, alone perform that change. Honors are conferred by service. The dignity of the spirit arises only from its natural growth, and those who strive to serve do so because they know of the happiness it will bring, not only in their world but in *ours*."[4]

Worldly rank and title are levelled; each must stand upon the foundations of his own character and development. While some mischievous spirits try sometimes to pose before inquirers, as being someone great or important, their deception is easily seen and known, on the spirit side of life. Many of the spirit counsellors, in telling of the life after death, speak of the period or "temple" of self-examination, to which we go after the passing. Here alone, in silence, and with memory of the past life most vivid, the soul reviews that life, as it passes in panorama before it, and judges and grades itself accordingly. Into this judgment is put, not only thoughts, words, and deeds, but also *motives*. And this we should remember, that *motives are important*, and as we strive for mastery let us examine our motives as well as our thoughts, words and deeds.

DWELLINGS IN THE SPIRIT WORLD:

Those who come back from the other side, to tell us of the homes over there, vary greatly in the description of these homes. This has a tendency to raise a doubt in the minds of many, as to the verity of the message. But the communicators tell us over and over again, to impress the fact on our minds, that, we do not all have the same kind or "degree" of home in the spirit world, any more than we do in this Earth world, since each one of us, largely builds his *eternal* home *there* during his life *here* while in the body. Our *home* in the spirit

---

[4] *The War Dead Return*, Barker.

world, is our *dwelling place* there, our *realm*, the right to which, we have earned while on the Earth-plane. According to our *consciousness* on this Earth-plane, is our dwelling-place in the spirit world, and as we progress in consciousness there, so are we able to go on and build "more stately mansions" for the soul.[5]

The following authoritative messages from the spirit-world will enlighten us:

"I found a home prepared for me in spirit life, but incomplete; I am now working to complete it. Every act of my earthly life, every secret thought, I found had taken tangible form. . . . During our sojourn on earth, our homes are prepared for us by the angels, and are built of the vibrations which go forth into the spiritual atmosphere from our hearts and lives. Will-power, when it subdues evil, beautifies the home.

"The smallest act of mercy, kindness, or compassion, of aid, of self-denial, of intellectual or bodily labor, to please, benefit or instruct others, will make its own beauty around the spirit, and will be found in some living object in the spirit home. . . . objects which are sources of satisfaction and joy.

"It should be remembered by the children of men, that it is not so much intellect on earth, as goodness, purity and self-sacrifice, that prepares the soul for the homes of the blest."[6]

Another great teacher and seer speaking from the spirit world says that what mortals need to fit them to heaven, or to build their "house not made with hands, eternal in the heavens" is "more trust in God, more faith in prayer, more true culture, more self-sacrifice, more of the attributes of humility, meekness, kindness, love, purity, honesty, serenity, justice, and truthfulness. . . . ."[7]

---

[5] *The Chambered Nautilus*, Holmes.

[6] *Immortality*, Peebles, 128, 138, 180.

[7] *Immortality*, Peebles, 234.

Our Ascent:

As cork rises in water to the extent of its buoyancy, so do the discarnate souls, almost as automatically ascend to that realm of the Astral World to which their degree of spiritual unfoldment, vibrations of thought, character and associations enable them to respond and affinitize. From that region they progress, to the still higher Realms, according to the efforts they make, and the degree of spiritual unfoldment they attain.

Conversely, all we have to do to contact the unseen worlds, is to raise the vibrations of our consciousness until it responds to the rate of the unseen realm we desire to contact, and since everything to which our consciousness responds is real to us while we are responding to it, when thus contacted, the unseen worlds become as real and substantial to us as is the physical world when we are responding to its lower octave of vibrations.

Desire Realm:

As the desire realm is the region to which the most undeveloped and least progressed souls are congregated,— including the atheist and the gross materialist—whose vibrations are slightly above the physical, they are able to exert great influence upon the lower and less developed class of people who are still on Earth. It is these vicious, and malign entities who are still seeking to express their evil tendencies on earth, by influencing those who are sensitive and respond to their forces, who are to a certain extent responsible for instigating our crime waves.

But again let us repeat: We do not have to contact or fight our way through the lower slums of the astral, unless something in us affinitizes us to them for a time until it is purged from us.

For sometime after we pass over, our after-life seems to be but a continuation of the interests of our Earth-life, and if our main thoughts and desires are still centered on Earth conditions, we naturally remain in the realm close to Earth, until we graduate from that realm and go higher.

WELCOMING COMMITTEE:

Death does not mean that we pass out into a vast realm or unknown region of darkness, uncertainty or loneliness, or even into a bright and shining heaven, or into a burning fiery hell. Usually we pass right into the arms of our loved ones.They know that we are about to graduate from Earth's common grade school, and so they gather as a reception committee, to greet and help us upon our arrival.

One voice from the spirit-world has said that the extrication of the spirit from the body is an office assigned to a certain order of angels. They receive souls kindly, and introduce them to their new sphere, where they quickly seek out those with whom they have an affinity. New-comers from the Earth rejoice at meeting their friends again, and their friends rejoice at their arrival. Husbands and wives meet and continue together for a long or short time according to their affinity.

Let us repeat the comforting assurance we give in the *Realms of the Living Dead*, page 49, that all that is necessary for your loved ones to be met by a reception committee, in the after-life, is for you to send out a strong mental wireless for the helpers, and they will be gathered to meet the newcomers.

WORKERS:

"After a few days of readjustment to the new surroundings, many of these new graduates join the great companies of unselfish servers who work to help the millions of other new arrivals, whose sudden thrust into the Astral World leaves them so confused that they cannot understand what has happened. These workers are organized in regiments, companies, and squads of rescuers, in which they work much

like the Red Cross woikers do here on Earth, giving ex-
planations, companionship and comfort to all who need
them."[8]

As reported by another authority: "In the first place,
when you come here, one of the things that astounds you
most, is the lack of difference. One of the first jobs is, to
meet the boys who have died in the war, suddenly, without the interim between the two consciousnesses, and to
explain to them what has happened and where they are."[9]

Guidance and enlightenment are needed over there,
even as they are here, and especially during the period immediately following the transition, before adjustment has
been made to the changed conditions. Those who make the
transition in love, are born into a new realization of love's
infinite capabilities, and its boundless building power.

Only one who is free from all such barriers, and who is
in very deed and truth a World Lover can become a leader,
teacher and liberator of such consciousness-bound egos.

One who has recently made the transition has been
called the "Friend of the World," and already he is engaged in work on the inner plane the scope and nature of
which is such as to amply justify the friendly appellation
thrust upon him.

The Grand Council:

The late President Roosevelt graduated from the conference of the Big Three statesmen into the Grand Council of
world statesmen, who are working not only for their own
nations, but for the best good of all. This Council includes
our former presidents, Washington, Lincoln, Harrison,
Qeveland, McKinley, Theodore Roosevelt, and Wilson, together with similar minded statesmen and former rulers of
other countries. There, with the wise assistance of the other
members of the Council, our late President will do his utmost to guide the decisions of our country, and influence for
the best the destiny of the world. His expert influence is so

---

[8] For further details, see *Realms of the Living Dead*, Curtiss, 48.
[9] *Unobstructed Universe*, White, 205.

plainly recognized that the newspapers write quite casually, "The man whose *Spirit-Presence* presides over this Conference, has been brought home to the onlookers ever since this parley started."[10]

ASSOCIATIONS:

The saying that "birds of a feather flock together" holds true even more forcibly over there than it does here on Earth. Your vibrations naturally affinitize you with like thoughts and desires. There can be no pretense or disembling over there, for your vibrations reveal exactly what you are, although there is much effort made to pose. But this cannot be done and thus your vibrations affinitize you with your kind almost as automatically as a dial telephone selects the numbers which you dial.

Unsympathetic members of an earthly family, coming into spirit life, automatically separate, each seeking congenial groups and societies. The law of attraction is the governing principle.

LONG SLEEP:

If, before you go over, you have a long drawn-out, exhausting illness, or have suffered much, you are usually given a protracted restful sleep. If you are a materialist, and do not believe in life after death, and go over under the influence of that thought, you will naturally be surrounded by clouds of such thought forms, and will remain in a state of coma until the amount of thought-force which you have put into the idea, has expended itself. This may take a thousand years or more, and then you will awaken and see how foolishly mistaken you have been.

Once we have been released from the bonds of the flesh, and accustomed ourselves to the conditions in the higher worlds, we find that the universal urge to eternal progress still prevails. We therefore desire to continue the unfoldment

---

[10] Washington Post, May 6ᵗʰ, 1945.

of our spiritual qualities, and to progress into an ever greater realization of our oneness with the Divine. We also seek to unfold all the qualities, which, by their practice, will enable us to be of greater service in whatever realm or region we find ourselves. Hence we occupy ourselves with those pursuits which facilitate our purgation, and therefore our advance.

CHILDREN MATURE:

The Law of Eternal Progress causes those who graduate from earth-life during childhood, to continue their growth until maturity, just as they would have had they remained here on earth.

As a noted spirit teacher has said: "The world calls me, — *us here* — dead. But sometimes people, unable to endure the thought of such a blanking out, speak of a loved one as having 'gone on.' That idea, the thought of going on, is more correctly true. It is true that we are *changed*; but so is man in his earth experience; changed from a new-born child to adulthood. And not only is he changed physically, but his perceptions are changed, his power of assimilation, his control of himself, and of the things of Earth about him."[11]

Since children have not had time to be greatly impressed with the more material conditions of earth-life, their minds remain pure and unsullied by the passions and gross selfish desires of the more mature life. Upon "graduation" they therefore naturally ascend into the higher realms of the astral life, to which the keynote of their characters affinitize them. There they are met by angelic spirit helpers, whose main delight is to work with and help children. They watch and wait for the coming of the children, that they may bear them tenderly to the rest homes, or schools, best fitted to their needs. "In the spirit world," says one writer, "I have seen the happy groups of children, frolicking, dancing, gathering flowers, listening to music, gaining instruction and unfolding in

[11] *Unobstructed Universe*, White, 33.

beauty and in life. Gleesome sounds burst from glad hearts—sweet lisps of affection, and the mischievous frolic of the child-heart. But around every child was an aura or a thread of life that connected it with the Earth so that it was to know where it was born and to tell each one's parentage. It was forever floating through the spirit atmosphere—the spirit forces of the parents went upward, and by natural law wound their life in and around the life of their little ones. This law is the result of affections, and if the child is loved but little, then the spirit law has severed the child from its parents' life, since it was by attraction,—which is love,—that the life of earth followed it away into the spirit world, and wound itself about the child of its love. There is no force used but a natural law of spirit—law of life.

"The spirit bodies of little children grow trancendently lovely. No human mind can conceive of the beauty and grace of these little ones. No unlovely object harms them— no frightful disease rends them. They unfold, as in spring the rosebud opens to the sun, or the petals of the lily unclose to the light of day. They all bear a semblance at first to their natural bodies; but as their souls grow and their spirits shine with the life of their souls, then they appear as their interior or mind makes them. The spirit body flows from the natural body. It is composed of its electric, magnetic, and spiritual life, and when first born into the spirit life, it has the exact form of the natural body. But as the grosser particles of its earthly magnetism are given off, and it becomes purer and truer, higher and holier, then it assumes a form of perfection and beauty. What the soul wills, or reveals, that is life and form and substance to the spirit.

"It often occurs that parents pass to the spirit world not long after their children, or perhaps at the same time. Being uninstructed in spiritual things, and ignorant of the spiritual laws, they are ill-fitted to develop the spiritual life of the child. Therefore, never mourn that you cannot go when your child goes. It has wiser nurses than you,—better teachers; if it has not more love, yet it has a higher love,—the love developed by wisdom."[12]

AGE DISAPPEARS:

On the other hand, those who graduate at an advanced age, gradually lose all trace of old age or disease, until they return to their most glowing stage of maturity, usually in the early thirties.

In a message recently received from Sir Oliver Lodge, after more than four years' experience in the after-life, to be sure of his facts, he corroborates our statement by saying, "I think you might say that I have knocked off about thirty, to thirty-five years, in appearance. The process of rejuvenation has been very easy."[13]

But if those in the spirit world return to communicate with those left behind on Earth, they must present themselves much the same as they looked when they graduated, or they would not be recognized. Likewise those who graduate in battle, or after operations, lose all trace of wounds, and regain their lost limbs, for the astral body is not mutilated by physcal operations.

PASSING IN BATTLE:

Those who pass on suddenly in battle find it difficult for a while to realize where they are. They know that they are not "dead," for they see their buddies and friends around them. And since they are clothed in astral duplicate of their uniforms, it is difficult for them to realize that they have lost their physical bodies. They realize that they have had some kind of physical shock, but they do not know just what has happened.

As we have explained elsewhere, "In the case of sudden death, either by accident or in the war, when the mind is still filled with the intense excitement of battle, the first awaken-

---

[12] *Immortality*, Peebles, 81-82.
[13] *Psychic News*, Sept. 8th, 1945.

ing often brings the soldier the sense of being suddenly
awakened from a dream, and he looks around in amaze-
ment for the familiar battle field. . . . With some few, the
force of the old hostilities and thoughts may for a time
impel them to hunt out and attack the enemy, and return
to the battle field on the physical plane. . . . But those in
the astral who keep on trying to fight are those who have
made themselves channels through which the evil astral
forces could express, and who were so filled with hatred
and lust for killing, that they desired to continue their habits of butchery after passing on. However, the majority
are met by their 'buddies' who have gone on before, and
are anxious to explain to the newly arrived, that for them
the fighting is over, for they have graduated into a higher
school of life."[14]

As an old friend has well said: "Soldiers who are hurled
from their physical bodies, while in the midst of battle
for their Fatherland, find themselves limited on the physical plane by boundaries corresponding to those that held
them nationally confined before crossing over. The joy
that comes with gaining the universal consciousness, is
not yet theirs."[15]

THE RETURN:

Since thought, desire, and love are even greater controlling factors over there than they are here, one of the first
impulses of the newly arrived is to contact their homes and
their loved ones. That strong desire naturally carries them
immediately to their homes over the magnetic current of
love connecting them with those left behind, and since they
are now still dose to Earth conditions, they often appear to
their loved ones in dreams or waking visions.

Although they cannot appear in physical form, they often
make their presence felt through currents of magnetism and
love. Since their dense astral bodies abstract heat and vitality
from the living, their first contact may cause a chill or shud-

---

[14] See *Realms of the Living Dead*, Curtiss, 68.
[15] *The New World Interpretation*, Corrine Dunklee.

der to pass over those living ones thus contacted. After a few such contacts, however, the chill becomes a thrill of recognition. Later a current of warmth, or a glow, may pass over the loved ones on Earth, as they respond, for as the astral body becomes purified and refined, it no longer causes chill.

DISAPPOINTMENTS:

These contacts are often ignored or shaken off by the living, either through lack of response, because they are not distinctly felt and recognized, or through fear due to ignorance, if they are felt. These rebuffs are a great disappointment to the departed ones. In fact it is as though they came home, and found nobody to respond to their knock at the door. If their presence is felt and response is refused, it is like slamming the front door in their faces.

YOUR RESPONSE:

While you may not dream about or feel the magnetic presence of the loved one, a thought of him may suddenly pop into your mind, when you have not been thinking of him, or something that he has said may suddenly occur to you. In such cases this is usually due to his concentrating his mind upon you, and your mind responds to his thought through mental telepathy. Since the fact of telepathy, or the direct exchange of thought from mind to mind, without physical contact, or the spoken or written word, has been so thoroughly demonstrated publidy to vast radio audiences, and otherwise, by the famous Mr. Dunninger, such exchange is no longer doubted, even if not thoroughly understood. And since the departed one still has his mind functioning perfectly, he can communicate through telepathy even more easily than he could when he was on the earth-plane. One test to determine whether it is really the loved one who is communicating is that his thoughts come into your mind in the characteristic way in which he would express them.

When you realize that any of these forms of conact are

being made, if possible stop whatever you are doing and pay attention, just as you would if the telephone or front door bell rang. Mentally say, "Yes dear one, I recognize your presence. Please stand outside my aura, and impress my mind with your message." Then proceed to talk with him as though he were upstairs, or in another room, out of sight but not out of hearing. In this way you can receive much love, comfort and guidance. It is in this way that God often uses our departed ones as messengers, to answer our prayers for comfort and guidance.

Be sure not to converse aloud with those in the unseen, unless you are alone, for persons overhearing you might think you are mentally unbalanced.

MAKING CONTACT:

One of the best ways to call a loved one with whom you wish to make contact is to use a photograph, one in which the eyes look directly at you if possible. As you send out your call, focus your gaze upon the pupils of his eyes while you smilingly pour a warm current of love into them, until he seems to smile back at you, or you feel the warm response which shows that a contact has been made. This same method has been used to comfort, heal, protect, and bless one who is still living in the flesh.

THEIR PROGRESS:

Remember that although your loved ones may keep in close contact mentally or telepathically for years, this need not keep them from progressing and graduating into the Higher Realms of light, peace, beauty and joy in spiritual activity into which their spiritual advance affinitizes them. Therefore do not hesitate to commune with them when you feel their presence or their thoughts, provided that you keep in mind that they are still fallible mortals and that their advice is no more reliable now than it was when they were on Earth, unless they have advanced in wisdom since passing on. Accept their advice only if it seems reasonable, and receives confirmation by a glow of warmth, a thrill, or a strong feeling of assurance or satisfaction from the Christ within.

And here we would like to quote a message from a spirit teacher as a warning which all those who are interested in spirit messages should heed:

"Remember that disorderly spirits, still sympathetically connected with the Earth, moving in your midst,. . . . are capable of doing great harm to humanity. They can commit actual sin through easy, negative-minded people upon the Earth. Changing worlds does not immediately change the desires of the miser, the thief or the carnally minded. These passions and tendencies do not pertain to the body,—*that* is material, unthinking, and irresponsible. It is the spirit that *thinks*, *wills* and *does* through the body; and it is the spirit whether it is in the body or out, that is normally responsible."[16]

Only the very lowest types of the returning spirits come back to prove any of the religious creeds, or to continue prejudice, revenge or hatred. The vast majority of those who return are glad to come, to give words of love, cheer and comfort to those left behind. The first thing they say is that they are happy that they can return, they still love those with whom they now talk, they see what is passing in their old homes, and they share the cares that were once theirs.

The father is still concerned about his children's welfare; the young lovers are still absorbed in their affection for each other; the mother is still the preserver and protector of the home.

PROTECTION:

To prevent you from being deceived by mischief-making, or malicious spirits in the astral, always use some prayer for protection, like our *Protecting Invocation* whenever commu-

---

[16] *Immortality*, Peebles, 166.

nicating. Owing to the war, conditions in the astral world are so confused and terrible that such protection is necessary daily, especially for all who are sensitive to invisible influence.[17]

The shedding of so much blood on the battle-fields feeds countless swarms of low type elementals in general. These elementals, together with great streams of thought—forms of horror, hatred, anger, revenge, and desire to kill—now reinforced by similar thoughts of both embodied and is-embodied Nazis and Japanese—form great whirlwinds of evil force to sweep over mankind. If you open the door to such forces by giving way more easily than formerly to irritation and anger, you may be overwhelmed by them into an outburst of temper far beyond that for which there is any excuse.

Also, if you feel unusually gloomy, discouraged or even physically tired and depleted, when there is no special physical or emotional reason, you may be reacting to these clouds of world evil which are not your own. In such cases, recognize the possibility and refuse to react, or give way to them, and protect yourself immediately with some protecting prayer.[17]

This chapter is written especially for the instruction and comfort of you who have lost loved ones, so that you may understand the condition of those who have graduated from this earth life. You can now look upon such transition, not as death, but as a graduation into a higher school in a continued, happier life in the higher worlds. Hence, services for such transition need not be regarded as a funeral but as graduation exercises. The departure of the loved one is just like that of one who has graduated from one phase of life, leaving home to go into another phase, excepting that he departs to enter life in the Higher Worlds. In short, he has *graduated* to another state of being, a *greater consciousness*, where, minus his cumbersome overcoat of flesh, he lives on; and *he*

---

[17] See *Dynamic Prayers*, Curtiss.

can come back to us to guide, protect, comfort, counsel, and encourage us, just as he did in the earth-life with us.

And let us repeat again for emphasis. Those who have gone over to the spirit world, *do live*, and *in their own individuality, consciousness, character and memory.*

CHAPTER IX

ANIMAL SURVIVAL

It will be a great comfort to many a sorrowing heart who has lost beloved pets, to know that there is ample physical proof of their personal survival after death. Not only is their presence often felt by their owners, but they have been photographed repeatedly. They have frequently manifested physically in materializing séances, where a dog's bark, a cat's call or a bird's chirp has been so plainly heard as to be positively identified by their owners.

TESTIMONY:

Many famous people have given their testimony to animal survival. Sir Arthur Oman Doyle has told how a medium coming into his study, clairvoyantly saw, and successfully described, the author's "dead dog" to him.

Sir Oliver Lodge has said that *affection is the most vital thing in life*, and like other vital realities, it continues on. The universe is governed by love more than anything else, and no reality of that kind fades out of existence. The higher animals have developed some human qualities, and have attained a stage at which there is individual memory, which is the beginning of personality. His dead son Raymond tells him that his favorite dog came to welcome him on his arrival in spirit land, and that he and others are not cut off from their animal friends.

WHERE ARE THEY?

Generally speaking, only domestic animals, who have acquired human qualities through their contact with man, return to demonstrate their *individual* survival of "death," but all species of animals when they die, go to the part of the spirit world known as the animal plane or sphere. They gravitate quite naturally to the environment most suited to their needs, state of consciousness and condition of passing.

"Some spirit people visit, and even live on the animal plane in order to work there. It all helps the sorrowing friends left behind to know that there is survival after death, and that even a beloved animal may be very much alive.

"Perhaps as compensation for the amount of wild animal life, thoughtlessly destroyed on earth, it might be a human's lot to render aid to the newly awakened spirits of slaughtered beasts. He may assist the bewildered cattle, recently slain, to become fully alive to their new form of existence. He may lead them to "pastures new" where contentment awaits them.

"In the perfect operation of divine law, both man and beast must receive compensation in the next sphere for what they have suffered on earth, as innocent victims of injustice."

GROUP-SOUL:

We are taught in our Cosmic Soul Science that all lower forms of life are but the expressions of the consciousness of one greater entity called the *Group-Soul*. Each species of animal has its own group-soul, which requires all the individuals of that group species to express its consciousness and to contribute to the evolution of the species as a whole. This groupsoul governs all its members by its consciousness, expressed as instinct.

Hence all members of the same species will automatically react in practically the same way, to any given set of conditions, unless they are more or less individualized by contact with mankind. It is only natural then, that upon their death, they should return to the realms in which the group-soul is located, thereby contributing to the consciousness of the whole, the result of their individual experience.

Even the very lowest forms of life have some sort of survival, because we know that the living spark cannot be extinguished by the death of the physical form, but, as we have said, the lower forms of animal life become a part of a group-soul when their physical life is over. But even this group-soul has its part to play in the operation of God's laws of evolution.

By losing its identity, and adding to the group-soul or "pool," the *one* is sacrified for the *whole*, and by the sacrifice of this *oneness*, not only is the group-soul advanced in evolution, but the *one* is raised nearer toward the stage, in its own evolution, where it leaves behind the animal consciousness, and is made ready for individuality of soul in a human form. The great spirit teacher, Silver Birch, to whom we have referred tells us. "There are two kinds of incarnation. There is the *old* soul, re-embodied in the world of matter, and there is the *new* soul starting its first phase in the world of matter, as a human individual."

ALL SURVIVE:

Although spirit communicators may not agree on all points, or certain points about the kind of survival of the more lowly forms of life, they agree on the fact of survival in some form or another, and on the points that matter. And as we have said before, they do all pass over to their own particular sphere on the animal plane. We are told that ferocious beasts do not continue to prey on other animals, because they do not feel the necessity of satisfying carnivorous appetites. For similar reasons the unpleasant characteristics of verminous pests cease to manifest.

NO BARRIERS:

While all animals have an after-life for a considerable period, in the case of wild animals, such survival occurs largely in the native habitat in which they lived before their death, and in groups and herds, such as those in which they lived on earth. This is for no great length of time, however, because they have not sufficiently developed the individuality from association with mankind, which the domestic animals have. In the case of pet animals, this same law of association, naturally draws them to their former masters. As one communicator says: "I want you to know, that death is not the end of all for your pet. Whenever you have a sense of needing him, your pet answers."

If the ties of love are very strong between you and your pet animal, you may expect it to be greeted by your friends on the other side upon its arrival. And, too, there are groups of animal-loving discarnate persons, who form a sort of rescue league, to look after pet animals, not able to make contact with their owners, left behind on the earth plane.

"Often, as on the Earth, an animal has to seek the aid of a human, before he can return from the spirit world, to his owners. As in the case of humans, *love* bridges the gap between the two worlds." And so it is only natural that those animals which have been closely associated with human beings should be so attracted to them after death, as to return and try to demonstrate their survival.

Psychic research, therefore, shows that there are no barriers to separate a human being and his animal friend, even if one is in the spirit world and one is here on the earth plane, if the association is mutually desired.

Materialization and Other Phenomena:

In the materializing séances of the Polish medium Kluski animals often appeared; the most frequent of these to materialize were dogs, cats and squirrels, while occasionally a large bird like a hawk or buzzard, and once even a tame lion appeared.

One of the buzzards was heard flying around the room, and beating its wings against the walls and ceiling, and *this bird was at one time photographed* by a magnesium flash. The séance was held in the light of a red lamp, fixed about six feet from the medium.

A few other examples drawn from the writings of an English investigator, who has given special attention to the subject, will illustrate the law:

In one materializing séance, the materialized form of a large dog suddenly appeared. He bounced forward in a most energetic manner, and proceeded to jump excitedly about the circle. Wagging his tail happily, he ran from one sitter to another, resting his paws on their knees, and sometimes licking a hand or face.

At another séance a small dog materialized sufficiently to bite playfully at the trouser legs and shoelaces of the owner.

Another instance of materialization and of direct voice is as follows: A Great Dane which, after a discarnate period of twenty years, often returned to its owner, barked so loudly through the trumpet that the owner said there was no mistaking its voice, and on other occasions it would plant its great paws heavily on her lap.

On several occasions a gentleman whose cattle dog had previously been killed, found when he went for his cattle, that the animals would begin to move and bunch together, as though the dog were there, helping to round them up as usual. This continued until he got another dog.

Four days after the death of her pet cat, the owner heard a thud on the bed and the sound of purring. There was the invisible cat greeting her from his old particular spot on the bed. Her husband heard the sound of the purring also, and quite distinctly. Later the same sound was heard by a visitor, who recognized it as that of the pet cat.

One dark night, as a gentleman was coming home from town along a lonely road, he heard a noise behind him, and turning around, he saw two men following him, apparently intent on robbing him. At the same moment a large black dog suddenly appeared at his side. With an oath the men slunk away. When the gentleman arrived at his gate he reached down and patted the dog, who had so adequately protected him, but while he was doing so, the animal dissolved into thin air.

A lady in Bath had a pet cat which was so jealous that it would never allow another cat to approach anywhere near its domain. Since its death the owner has tried to keep many cats, but none would stay but for a short period. The owner considered this evidence of her jealous pet's still dominating its neighborhood. A few days after the same cat passed on, it manifested itself to its owner by jumping from its accustomed resting place and pattering over to her. The jump down and the patter of the feet, were so loud as to be distinctly heard by others in the next room.

Through the trumpet a guide told a sitter of the presence of a black sheep dog, called Rough. Its owner testified that this dog had been raised from a puppy, and had passed away some time previously. Its name was Rough as correctly stated by the guide.

The author had a very large, very heavy cat, whose favorite resting place was a certain chair, which it refused to vacate until it was tilted so that it had to jump to the floor with a characteristic thump. After the passing of this cat, the chair in which it had been known to sit, would frequently be so heavy, that it could scarcely be moved until it was tilted forward. As soon as this occurred the familiar thump on the floor could be heard, and the chair could then be easily moved.

At a home materializing séance, a large dog often materialized, resting his paws on the knees of the sitters. The crowning manifestation occurred, when on one occasion he ran to a bowl of water which had been provided at the séance for psychic purposes, and began to lap up the water eagerly and noisely, as though the excitement had made him thirsty. Afterwards the bowl was found to be completely empty and there was not a drop of spirit water to be seen.

PLATE II—A "dead" puppy appeared as a psychic extra when this
photograph of his wolf-hound friend was taken.

PLATE III—A medium and her psychic friends.

PHOTOGRAPHY OF ANIMALS AFTER DEATH:

There are many incidents authoritatively cited of photographs of animals after death, sometimes when the photographer was trying to get pictures of human beings from the spirit land. In one instance the medium took the photograph but instead of the expected relative, there appeared on the plate an "extra" of a terrier Floss, a pet of the medium which had died a short time before.

In another case where a woman was trying to get a spirit picture of a dead relative there appeared instead, one of a pet cat, which had been dead a week only. On the same photograph there was seen also the words, "Dear Parents," written by the child of one of the sitters. This child was in the spirit world, and the owner of the pet was told that it was being looked after by the child, who had written a long message to her parents in minute but clear writing.

At another time in the photograph of a medium and others at the seashore, there appeared, not only the picture of the dead son of the medium, but also one of a pony who had passed on and who had been loved and owned by the son.

In the picture shown here of a woman and her Irish wolf-hound, is found the very dear and easily discernible picture of a puppy. The owner of the wolf-hound recognized the puppy as one which had died a short time ago, and to which both she and the wolf-hound had been deeply attached. The puppy had been in the habit of lying down with him, with its head in the same position as it is in the picture.

The other picture shown is a reproduction of a spirit picture taken over eighteen years ago. The spirit individuals plainly visible around the medium, have been identified. They are, starting at the top and going left to right—Hanniah, Hindu Control; the medium's dog which was killed in an automobile acddent; Patha, materialization helper and chemist; Georgiana, child guide and message bearer; Professor Iran, Philosopher and Teacher; Dr. Benjamin, Spirit Chemist; and Timothy, trumpet control. This picture is reproduced from *The Psychic Observer*.

These are just a few of the many cases on record of spirit photographs of animals, which have been taken.

The cases and the picture on Plate II, are taken from *When Your Animal Dies*, by Sylvia Barbanell. For other cases and details see this splendid book.

With this widely attested-to array of physically proven facts, there should no longer be any doubt left in the unprejudiced mind as to the reality of animal survival of bodily death.

SUPER INTELLIGENCE OF ANIMALS:

That some animals possess an intelligence away above the average of their species, has been proven in many cases. Their mental powers have been investigated, studied and written about by scientists, professors, savants and psychologists. They have demonstrated qualities of reason, humor, and sometimes a certain psychic ability, and that they have memory and powers of reflection. In addition, some of these animals have solved problems of arithmetic which have been confusing to many a mathematically informed human.

Properly trained horses can spell and work out mathematical problems by the stamping of their hoofs, or by picking out strips of wood, on which were stamped letters, even to the extraction of the cube root. Maeterlinck, that profound thinker, poet and writer; that blend of mystic sense and scientific spirit, once paid a visit to the stables of the famous Elberfield horses, and found that one of them solved problems of mathematics which stumped even the great man himself.

A Shetland pony, Black Bear, was owned and trained by Mr. Barrett of New York. Black Bear's unexpected replies to questions, showed almost independent thinking, and sometimes his knowledge of historical events surpassed what had been taught him. He seemed to develop an intuitive proficiency in the subjects which had been taught him, far surpassing that of his master, who was often perplexed by the variety of information, mathematical skill and imaginative powers displayed by the pony.

The authority referred to in this chapter, further says; "There is testimony available regarding this intelligence, of over sixty animals — including forty-four dogs — who had learned to 'speak' their thoughts understandingly by means of an alphabetical code taught them by their owners.

After they had mastered the alphabet, and learned to count, the dogs were able to convey their own thoughts, either by tappng their paws, by barking or by other methods. Thus they could converse and exchange points of view with their human friends. . . . ."

Cracker, a dog, saved the life of his owner's daughter. The child was seen by the dog to be clinging to the back of her father's moving car. In order to attract the owner's attention, Cracker threw himself repeatedly at the car. He died from the injuries received, but his efforts succeeded in saving the life of the child.

There are people who keep a cat merely for catching mice, but anyone who has had experience in treating a cat as a member of the family, knows that this animal has intelligence and seeming reasoning power. The cat, though seldom as demonstrative as a dog, is capable of deep affection.

"Nurse Nichols" was preparing breakfast, when she heard a tapping on the window pane. A kitten was by this means trying to attract her attention. She followed the animal into the garden, where it led the way to a shed. Here the nurse found the gardener suffering from a stroke. Normally no one would have gone to the shed until evening, by which time it would have been too late to save the life of the stricken man.

A great number of other stories of the reasoning power of cats have been recorded.

Birds also come into their share of credit for intelligence which seems almost human in its scope and stories are told of birds being jealous, and refusing to sing when a strange bird was brought into the room; and of exhibiting other marked evidences of intelligence, above that of the ordinary animal.

On the Radio program, "We The People," there was featured a parrot, which after twenty years of close association with its master, exhibited such human intelligence as to give surprisingly intelligent answers to the questions asked by the audience.

Even with non-domestic animals, it has been found that, when in constant contact with humans, they develop intelligent observation, and they acquire "personalities" of their own.

A ship stationed in Fort Blair Harbor was dressed for the celebration of the captain's birthday party, with flags and bunting. Trained elephants were at work on the shore, handling timber, and soon came a message from the shore with orders to undress the ship of its flags and decorations. The elephants saw them and sensing a holiday, refused to work.

The examples given above will serve to illustrate this absorption of human intelligence, by animals of different kinds. (Unless otherwise especially assigned, the quotations and examples in this chapter are from the splendid book on this ubject. *When Your Animal Dies*, by Sylvia Barbanell, as we have previously noted.)

ENSOULMENT:

We feel that a word of warning should be issued as to certain dangers involved in making an animal too intimate a member of the family, for by so doing we assume considerable responsibility for that animal's evolution.

All living things are constantly throwing off emanations of various kinds. With human beings these include bodily, astral, psychic, mental and spiritual emanations. These impinge upon, and are absorbed by, everything within their environment. Because of this the trained psychomotrist can pick up their vibrations, and thus determine whatever form of life and activity had been present at any certain place.

When great love and affection are given to an animal, these emanations are focussed more forcefully on that animal. As the animal unconsciously absorbs more of them, it naturally becomes more than a mere animal, to the degree to which it is able to absorb them. In other words to that extent the animal becomes humanized. This plainly shows in the superintelligence displayed by these specially gifted animals, mentioned elsewhere in the chapter. These animals have received intensive training by their owners, and thus they have absorbed so much of their trainers' mental emanations, that their consciousness is expanded beyond that of the animal, until their minds are partially humanized. Hence they frequently have the reasoning and deductive powers of a twelve year old child or beyond, for they live in the intellectual world of man, instead of the instinctive world of animals.

This humanization of the animals, by the absorption of human emanations, can be carried to the extent of practically *ensouling* them with a part of the human soul vibration. This makes the animal more than animal, and to that extent, humanized, and takes it out of its normal evolution, and from under the guidance of its group soul. It may even reincarnate more than once in this life and also be sufficiently humanized to reincarnate with you, in a future life. Hence you become responsible for its future evolution, until the development of its human qualities enables it to enter the human kingdom. Thus, long after you have become superman and no longer have to incarnate on this planet, you will have to look down on, guide and be responsible for the evolution of this animal, as its "Father-in-Heaven," until it becomes an individualized human being. You should therefore, think well before you assume such a responsibility.

Even in the case of non-domestic animals, it has been found that when close contact with humans has been established, intelligent observation develops, and they acquire personalities of their own.

In the recent publication of Anice Payson Terhune's, *Across the Line*, spoken of in another chapter, she speaks of asking her husband on the other side, if the dogs are there with him and he replies:

"Laddie and Wolf knew me at once. It was so good to have them bounding around me again."

Here we have the word of one who was deeply interested in religious subjects and the life on the other side of "the Line," before his going over, that animals do live and have consciousness after they leave this Earth-plane.

Chapter X

THEOSOPHISTS' CLAIMS

Many of our philosophical friends disapprove of all attemps to communicate with our departed loved ones, and in many cases look down on spiritualists with a "holier than thou" attitude, as being ignorant of the true occult philosophy back of spiritualistic phenomena.

However this undercurrent of misinterpretation of motives, is fast being dissipated, until today there seems to be a greater understanding between these two great Schools of Thought.

We find the Canadian Theosophist of July 1942, stating that—"Spiritists have long ago demonstrated the reality of socalled 'independent writing.' That it was done by 'dead people' is a contradiction in terms. Without the intense vitality such a thing could never be done. Beside, there are no 'dead' beings; for there is no death."

It is only natural that the modern generation of Theosophists should be ignorant of the conditions under which the Society was founded, unless they have given special study to its origin. Hence they would not know that their founder, Madame Helena Petrovna Blavatsky, one of the most remarkable women, and one of the greatest religious awakeners, who is known among us chiefly through her efforts to establish in the Occident the philosophy of the Orient,—*Theosophy*,—also recognized Spiritualism as a great religious truth, which is proved by its phenomena. When Madame Blavatsky,—commonly referred to as H.P.B.,—arrived in New York penniless and alone, away back in 1873, the first contacts she sought out were among the Spiritualists. Among these early contacts were the well known mediums, Nelson and Jennie Holmes of Philadelphia. She next visited the Eddys at Chitenden, Vermont. To a friend in Russia she wrote:

"I am going to visit next from here, a family of strong psychical mediums, and stay among them for some time; they are the Eddys, and I shall make experiments for myself and, if satisfactory, I will use them in my work for the enlightenment of mankind. There is no doubt that the coming avatars and teachers must incorporate in their philosophy, this crowning revelation of the age, modern Spiritism." [1]

Colonel Olcott, the co-founder with H.P.B. of the Theosophical Society, pays this glowing tribute to her mediumship. "I gradually discovered that this lady, whose brilliant accomplishments and eminent virtues of character, no less than her exalted social position, entitle her to the highest respect, is one of the most remarkable mediums in the world." [2]

Madame Blavatsky also attended materializing séances given by the medium Dr. Henry Slade, at the home of E. Furness in Philadelphia. Among the many types of phenomena which were produced, were lengthy messages precipitated upon slates, in several languages, which her great linguistic ability and trained intellect could readily translate and appreciate, since she had learned some forty languages.

In fact it was at a séance with Dr. Slade, that she received her first written word of encouragement, from her Masters, since reaching America, in a slate-written message. Part of the message read as follows: "The Masters are behind the whole world of spirits and mortals." [3]

It was after this heartening message that she is quoted as saying; "I am ready to sell my soul for Spiritualism, but nobody will buy it." [4]

---

[1] *Psychic Observer*, May 10th, 1943.
[2] *Peoples From Other Worlds*, Olcott.
[3] *Psychic Observer*, May 10th, 1943.
[4] *Psychic Observer*, May 10th, 1943.

PLATE IV—Buckle and Medal of H.P.B.'s Father.

Modern students do not realize that H.P.B.—was a powerful materializing and apport medium. At an early séance with the Slades, there was apported into her hand, a buckle, and one of her father's war medals, both of which had been placed in his coffin when he was buried years ago. This was brought psychically, by her deceased uncle, whom she had seen materialized that evening.

Colonel Alcott, who was present asked. "Was there ever a manifestation more wonderful than this? A token dug by unknown means, from a father's grave and laid in his daughter's hand, five thousand miles across an ocean."[1]

On one occasion Madame Blavatsky held in her right hand, a blue sapphire ring belonging to her visitor Mrs. Carmichael. This lady expressed a desire that the ring be duplicated if possible, in order to demonstrate the presence and power of the Mahatmas of H.P.B. After an interval of a minute or two, H.P.B. extended her hand saying, "Here is your ring," showing at the same instant *two* sapphire rings, the one belonging to Mrs. Carmichael, and the other one identical in every respect, except that the second one was larger and with a better cut stone. "Why do you give me this," said Mrs. Carmichael, in surprise. "I have not done it, it is a gift from the Mahatmas," answered H.P.B.

At another occasion, at a dinner party, at the first command of Madame Blavatsky, there came rushing through the air her tobacco pouch, box of matches, her pocket handkerchief, or anything she asked for or was made to ask for.

"Her powers manifested themselves as incessant knocks, raps and other sounds, the moving about of furniture without contact, and the increase and decrease of the weight of various objects.

"It is far easier to enumerate the phenomena that *did not* take place during these memorable hours, than to describe those that did."[2]

---

[1] *Peoples From Unseen Worlds*, Olcot, 338.
[2] *Incidents In the life of Madame Blavatsky*, Sinnett, 107, 260.

On many occasions she materialized letters from her Masters in India. They appeared materialized on the ceiling, and then dropped to the floor, in the presence of one or more other persons.

ASTRAL CORPSES:

Theosophists claim that the mediums do not make contact with the soul of the deceased, but only with its astral corpse. While it is true that the Spirit does ultimately graduate out of the astral world into the mental world and thereby leaves behind his astral body, as an empty shell or astral corpse, as a rule this does not take place for many years, at least until most of his loved ones left behind on Earth have also graduated into the astral world to join him. Therefore, usually, there would be no astral shell for them to contact before they also made the transition.

REASONING POWERS LACKING:

While it is also true that should such an astral corpse be contacted before it is too greatly disintegrated, it is possible for its astral brain to be temporarily vitalized by the forces of the medium and the inquirer, so that it might repeat some of the most vivid impressions made upon it, during life, automatically, like a phonograph record, yet it would not possess intelligence enough to carry on a conversation or answer questions, requiring the power of reasoning, for the remaining Ego has withdrawn from it.

Also, it is extremely unlikely that such an astral corpse would be allowed to drift into a well organized séance, for any responsible manager—commonly called a Guide—of the astral side of the séance is very careful to select only those he allows to enter the group that will try to communicate through the medium.

SELDOM ENCOUNTERED:

Also such astral corpses usually disintegrate rapidly unless they are grossly animal and densely material. In our more than thirty years of psychic research we have never encountered such an astral shell, although we have encountered diakkas, or man-made elementals in human form.

MME. BLAVATSKY'S WARNING:

The theosophical attitude is probably due to the fact that Madame, in her great desire to prevent negative and unselfreliant persons from continually running to mediums—especially those mediums who are untrained and only partially developed,—for advice on their daily affairs, discouraged with a warning to her followers, that it was possible that an astral shell might be encountered. Her great desire evidently, was to turn attention from the transient phenomena to the eternal philosophy.

MR. SINNETT'S STATEMENT:

Another factor is the reckless and wholly unsupported statement of Mr. Sinnett, made without the slightest reference to evidence, to say nothing of proof, that "such an empty shell is the angel guide of the average medium," made toward the close of the last century—(1882)—before modern psychical research had really begun. Such a statement is now as entirely out of date as were any conceptions of radio activity the world may have had at that time. But naturally statements made by earlier writers, are taken for granted by later followers, hence discourage their personal investigations in the light of modern science. But no matter who makes such sweeping statements without giving the proof of their authenticity they are definately disproved by modern scientific psychic research as reported herein.

BECOME SELF-RELIANT:

Since the most important reason for our incarnating here on Earth is to learn to follow the guidance of the Christ within in making our own decisions, the continual running to mediums for advice would weaken our characters, and make us "leaners" instead of masters of our actions, we too discourage such dependence upon our departed friends. But this does not mean that we cannot have friendly visits with them from time to time, just as we might call on them for a social evening, were they still on Earth.

To teach that it is only the empty shells of our departed loved ones that are contacted by mediums is a great mistake, due to a lack of the Theosophists' full understanding of their own philosophy. Even Madame Blavatsky's own Master, Koot Hoomi Lal Singh—usually referred to as K.H.—distinctly says that the Egos of our departed loved ones are contacted by those left behind, through the proper use of well developed mediums.

Sinnett's Claims:

On this subject Mr. A. P. Sinnett remarked: "The remarks appended to a letter in the last Theosophist, strike me as very important and as qualifying—I do not say contradicting—a good deal of what we have been told hitherto, *in re* Spiritualism. We have heard already of a spiritual condition of life in which the redeveloped Ego enjoyed a conscious existence for a time before reincarnation; but that branch of the subject has hitherto been slurred over. Now some explicit statements are made about it."

To this the Master Koot Hoomi replied as follows: "The Souls of pure, loving sensitives think their loved ones come down to them on earth, while it is their Spirits that are raised toward those in Deva-Chan. Many of the subjective communications—most of them when the sensitives are pure minded—*are real*; but it is most difficult for the uninitiated medium to fix his mind on the true and correct pictures of what he sees and hears. Some of the so called psychography—slatewriting or precipitated handwriting (the more rarely)—*are also real*. The Spirit of the sensitive getting odylized, so to say, by the spirit in Deva-Chan, becomes for a few minutes that departed personality, and writes in the handwriting of the latter, in his language and in his thoughts, as they were during his life time. The two spirits become blended into one; and the preponderance of the one over the other during such phenomena, determines the preponderance of the personality in the characteristics exhibited in such writing and 'trance speaking.' What you call 'rapport' is in fact an identity of molecular vibration between the astral part of the medium and the astral part of the discarnate personality. . . . And the question whether the communication shall reflect more of one personal idiosyncrasy or the other is determined by the relative intensity of the two sets of vibrations in the compound wave of *Akasa*. The less identical the two sets of vibrations, the more mediumistic and the less spiritual will be the message. So then measure your medium's 'moral state' by that of the alleged 'controlling intelligence' and your tests of genuineness leaves nothing to be desired." [3]

THEOLOGICAL MISCONCEPTIONS:

Through similar misunderstandings, fundamentalist theologians have published some pamphlets and books composed of quotations from the Bible, referring to life after death. The quotations purport to *prove* that the "dead know nothing," and include the doctrines of literal hell-fire, eternal punishment, and the monstrous doctrine of infant damnation. The literal and materialistic interpretation of such allegorical passages, is quite as erroneous as similar passages quoted by the early church-fathers in the days of Galileo, which seemingly proved that the Earth was flat and did not circle round the sun. These quotations about life after death, are just as misconceived, and equally as erroneous, as were those concerning the shape of the Earth and its revolutions around the sun, for modern psychic research has just as definitely refuted them, with physical proofs, such as are presented herein, as Galileo refuted the claims of the early church-fathers.

---

[3] *The Mahatma Letters*, Sinnett, 99–103.

Therefore those who deride or oppose Spiritualism, perhaps unwittingly or through ignorance, are going against the plain teachings of their founder and her Masters. They have much to learn about our connection with our discarnate friends, and should be open-minded enough to drop their unfounded prejudices, and accept the scientifically proven facts, instead of clinging blindly to misconceived theories, which have been so completely disproved by modern scientific research.

CHAPTER XI

A MESSAGE FROM MADAME BLAVATSKY

Transcribed by

DR. AND MRS. F. HOMER CURTISS

*Founders of The Universal Religious Fellowship, Inc.
Authors of "The Curtiss Books"*

The many messages from Madame Blavatsky given to the authors in her own handwriting and over her own identified signature, as reproduced in this volume, should be sufficient evidence of the close contact the authors have had with her through many years. These messages should be sufficient evidence too, of the authenticity of the following message, dictated to Mrs. Harriette Curtiss by Madame Blavatsky, Oct. 16th, 1928.

This message was given to the transcribers some time ago for a special purpose. But the Author of the message now directs them to make it public. And they herewith comply with that instruction, that the message may reach the hearts of those who are ready for it.

———

CURTISS PHILOSOPHIC BOOK CO.

Washington, D. C.

It is very important that there should be a plain understanding of my teachings on some of the subjects which are
causing so much misunderstanding among my followers
in other societies, so that you can put things in a plain and
definite way which will carry conviction, and will help,
we hope, to bridge the chasm of separation and bring us
all closer together as one family sitting at the table of our
Father. You will have difficulty in making certain ones
comprehend, owing to their fixed idea that only the ex-
planations given them by their so-called authorities can be
accepted. But I want this my explanation written out so that
those to whom it is shown can accept it or not; then at least
we have done our part in presenting the truth.

At the time when she who was known as Helena Petrovna
Blavatsky was on earth, although she had many faults and
many misconceptions she was nevertheless chosen for the
great work of preparing the Western world for the coming
of the Great Teacher, the Avatar. She was never worthy
in her own eyes, except in the sense that she was willing
to take up the burden and would not lay it down until the
work was accomplished. The chief work that she gave to
the world, *The Secret Doctrine*, was made up largely from
the Ancient Teachings, the fundamental principles of the
Wisdom-Religion. These were gathered from the Ancient
Teachings because there they were most accessible, and
because they expressed most convincingly the essential
principles of that religion. So with many a self-interpolated
dictum and with many a hammer and tongs she did the best
she could. And what has been the result?

With great suffering and many mistakes the Theosophical
Society was founded. And finally the time came for her to
lay down the outer part of her physical work. But did she
lay it down altogether? No. That was impossible, because
when one is chosen and given a definite work to do for the
Masters in a definite cycle, that work must come under the
Great Law.

And one is never chosen and then the work pushed on him,

but the choice always results because in his past incarnations he himself has asked for the opportunity and has tried to prepare himself, has literally said: "Here am I, use me!"

She was chosen as a Messenger of the Lodge because she had that karmic right and had sought to prepare herself for that work. And it is well to understand clearly what I mean by a Messenger of the Lodge. The Lodge has messengers of greater or lesser degrees, but all messengers must be in conscious touch with the Lodge and be willing to lay down their own personalities, their own lives, to do the Master's work and must be those whose Karma permits this. And yet at certain eras in the world's history, when we might say the world is approaching a great event, such as the descent of the Avatar, there is always some special Messenger sent out who has the characteristics, force and power to hew the way like John the Baptist; to make straight His paths, to prepare for His coming.

This preparation for the coming of the Great Teacher could not be accomplished merely by gathering together a few followers to study the philosophy of the Ancient Teaching's; they had been studied for ages. How hopeless such a task! You know how even during her life time she had few friends. Her true friends she could count on the fingers of her hand, or on both at best. She had no one who was really close, who really understood her or comprehended her *real mission*. She was either regarded as a mountebank and a doer of wonders, hence sought out for pastime and entertainment, or as a half-crazed enthusiast who was trying to make a stir in the world by putting forth bizarre doctrines which would upset the placid faith of easy going Christianity which had only just settled down into a comfortable jog-trot after the strenuous experiences of persecution and intolerance of past ages. People either fawned on her or flattered her and demanded her help or they derided. And oh, how they crushed and trampled on her highest ideals and belittled her great mission!

At last there came a time, as there always does, when the

Great Ones said; "Dear child, you have worked long enough under this terrible handicap of disbelief, of bickering, of criticism. Now you can continue your work where it will be easier; where you can stand aside, can look at the Teachings you have given out, and at the Source from whence you gathered them, and can understand more fully what is still necessary for the coming age." So Mme. Blavatsky, according to the world's opinion, died, and according to the ideals of the Theosophical Society was transplanted into a higher sphere of activity where she would still be capable of carrying on her work.

According to the very teachings which had been so carefully gathered and inculcated in the little group which at that time called itself the Theosophical Society, it had been pointed out that when a Teacher has accepted the great responsibility of preparing for the coming of an Avatar, such a Teacher never goes into Devachan or accepts Nirvanic bliss; that always, if he is worthy the name of Agent, he makes the great sacrifice and remains in the Earth's aura and in close touch with his followers to teach and help them and to watch over the seed he has planted and help it to continue its growth. This teaching is scattered all through her writings.[1] When

---

[1] Among the many such references we call attention to the following: "Of the voluntary and conscious incarnations of Adepts there are two types, those of Nirmanakayas, and those undertaken by probationary chelas who are on their trial. . . . There are cases—rare, yet more frequent than one would be disposed to accept – which are the voluntary and conscious reincarnations of Adepts on their trial. . . . But few are those who outside the higher degrees of adeptship, can guide the latter (astral body), or any of the principles that animate it, when once death has closed their short terrestrial life. *Yet such guidance. . . . is not only possible but is of frequent occurance.* . . . After the physical translation of such a Saint. . . . his astral principles cannot be subjected to a natural dissolution like those of any common mortal. They remain *in our sphere and within human attraction and reach.* . . . Such an adept *remains in the astral plane connected with our Earth*, and henceforth moves and lives in the possession of all his principles except the Kama-Rupa and physical body. . . . Those are Adepts who give up Nirvana for the sake of helping humanity. . . . This kind of easy death. . . . symbolizes the "death" of any Adept who has reached the power and degree and also the purification which enables him to "die" in the physical body, *and still live and lead a conscious life* in his astral body." (*The Secret Doctrine,* Vol 2, 559; Vol. 3, 365-67, 372.) Other references are too numerous to mention. H.P.B. promised never to come back "as a spook," and she never has, but this does not mean that she has not continued to work, through the independent or telepathic method (See *Realms of the Living Dead,* Curtiss, 225), through enlightened and devoted followers who are so developed and trained as to respond to her direc-

they cry, "Back to Blavatsky" why do they not go back to her fundamental teachings on *this* subject as well as others?

There never has been a great Teacher or a Messenger who, after he put away the hampering body of flesh, does not remain close to his pupils; who does not continue his work; does not come and appear to and speak with his followers. To say that Mme. Blavatsky died and then disappeared and left her work, left it in the chaotic and undeveloped and unfulfilled condition you all know it was in, and is still in today, is simply to deny her the one little recognition of her work that at least her followers should be glad to give her, namely, that she was an authorized agent and Messenger of the Lodge. For, as I have said, if she laid down her work at death she broke the Law. And if she had not been a Messenger she would have been repudiated long before her death. This doctrine of "the self-sacrifice of one who voluntarily gives up the absolute Nirvana in order to help humanity and be still doing it good. . . . to save his fellow-creatures *by guiding them*"[2] has been plainly given to the Theosophical Society. And the Masters of Wisdom, be They of high or low degree, far advanced or only a few steps on the Path of Mastery, all obey this Law. Therefore, being an Agent of the Lodge, "an Adept on his trial," she also could be expected to obey this Law.

Is it conceivable that the great Masters of Wisdom and Compassion who knew that the whole Earth was about to pass its great baptism of horror and of blood and of dissolution; who knew that the days foretold from the beginning of time; were about to be entered upon; who knew that this poor little Earth was about to pass through its most terrible time of testing; is it conceivable that these Great Souls would say: "Yes, we know that the world is about to reach its darkest night; we know that war and fire and sword and famine, pestilence, desolation and horror are stalking abroad. But we will now withdraw our Messenger and let no one from the Lodge

---

tions, not in any kind of trance or "spook control" *but in full waking consciousness*. The evidence is too plain to be ignored.

[2] *The Secret Doctrine*, Blavatsky, iii, 366

interfere to help or comfort or guide. Let the poor suffering little children fight it out alone with what we have already given them. We will do no more to help. There will be no one sent from the Lodge until 1975 when it is all over! We will remain away in hiding, in some safe retreat where we cannot be hurt while they die and starve and suffer and sink down into a hopeless hell in the horrors they must face." I say is this conceivable?

Is there a person living, especially one who calls himself a theosophist, who can so belittle and falsify the teachings and condemn the great loving Masters who, as they have been taught, are the "guardian wall" around humanity, who are the givers of compassion and love, and the "watchers through the night," the great lovers of mankind? Yet, apparently this is the result of Mme. Blavatsky's teachings. Oh, if such a horrible doctrine were true, I myself would gather the peoples of the earth together and I would say: "Find these so-called Masters of Wisdom and tear them limb from limb and throw them to the dogs! Find this God of theirs in his highest heaven and tear him down, and say to this God: How dare you make man and then leave him helpless and without comfort to suffer and die under such terrible conditions! How dare you!" Yet this is what my followers today are saying that Mme. Blavatsky taught! Ah, my children, it is unthinkable! It is monstrous! It is villainous! It is horrible!

On the contrary, according to the Great Law, when a Messenger of the Lodge is given a work to do upon the earth plane, and owing to his Karma, his disposition, his racial characteristics and to a thousand other factors, he fails to a certain extent to carry out his mission as well as he should, and yet his heart is true and he wants to do better, he is taken up into a higher realm, yet not far from Earth, and there is given an opportunity to do better, to see more clearly, to work harder, to correct mistakes, and to make the great renunciation of Nirvanic bliss to remain as the guardian and guide of his followers: for he would not lay down his advanced state to incarnate again as a babe, and thus waste the most precious years of the cycle while waiting to grow up to an age at which he could resume his work.

Again, they say that granting that all this is so, why could not some one in the great and loving and brotherly Theosophical Society be chosen to carry on her work? Oh, they are doing it beautifully, are they not? But I tell you now that there is absolutely not one among all the T. S. members in the world whom, if he will come to me and listen to me and obey me, I will not teach and help and inspire; who, if he will let go his own preconceived ideas of what Theo-sophia is, I will not guide and enlighten. But they will not. They will not realize that when on Earth Mme. Blavatsky gave out but the outer body of the Mystic Teachings or Theosophy, the shell let us say. But now, like all such Teachers, when she has entered into *her real work* upon a higher plane, she has to take that outer shell and build into it its soul, the Mystic Teachings of the Heart-Doctrine, the love, the understanding, the sympathy and the personal touch, because today that is what the world needs.

In those early terrible days of materialism the world needed hammer blows, needed to be shown that real religion, the Wisdom Religion, was scattered through all religions; needed to be shown that even those religions which they called "heathen" contained the mighty spiritual truths needed to guide the life. This was acomplished, but after she had passed out the world had changed. It was no longer merely materialism we had to fight. The world was seeking and crying out for truth, for love, for understanding, for brotherhood. Therefore, as the dark night came upon the world it had to have the inner side of the teachings, especially the inner side of the Christian teachings, explained to it. But where could I find anyone with mind open enough and who were karmically prepared to give these except the simple ones I chose?

Therefore I say let all those who consider themselves true

theosophists turn aside from worshipping the outer shell of the teachings and seek the heart. Let them say: "Yes, all that former teaching was necessary and fundamental and is good, but can it alone really help us in these days of misery and unrest? Can philosophy alone really feed our Souls? Yet, we know that in Theosophy, *real Theosophy*, there is this Bread of Life. But who shall break it and give it to us? Where are the disciples who can take the five loaves and the two small fishes and give them to the multitude?" When they have said this let them take the Mystic Teachings I have more recently inspired [3] and see if they cannot find in them the real inner nourishing food of *true* Theosophy; not the exact interpretation perhaps, not the talk, not the controversy, not the arguments, but the spirit; the Spirit of Truth; the help, and the understanding of humanity which needs different treatment today than it needed when Mme. Blavatsky was on earth in the flesh.

Not until the work of that Teacher is accomplished will she take her rest. And it will never be accomplished until the inner Mystic Spirit of her teachings has been given out. And when I say the inner Mystic Spirit I mean the things which touch the heart, which grip the understanding, which help men and women to live in spite of the hard times; to stand up and face themselves and the world in spite of all the things they are passing through today, rather than mere metaphysical speculations and disrupting, hair-splitting disputations over doctrinal points. Her work will never be accomplished until it has brought out the true religion within the framework of the philosophy or outer body of the theosophical doctrine; until it has shown the great spiritual power, not only in the ancient religions, but also *that same identical spiritual power and those same truths in the Christian religion.*

In the days when Mme. Blavatsky was on Earth the Western world believed in what was called the Christian religion, but could not believe that one could be anything but a

---

[3] Teachings of *The Universal Religious Fellowship, Inc.*

"heathen" who could see truth in any other religion. It was the work of Theosophy *at that time* to bring the truth of other religions to the attention of the Christian world. And this work has been so well accomplished that as a result today it is a common thing for people to go to the Hindus and the philosophies of other ancient peoples and pick out their wonderful pearls of great price. Many of such persons say that Christianity is a failure; that there is nothing in it. Therefore Mme. Blavatsky has not finished her work until she brings the same understanding of the Christian Mysteries to the public mind that she brought to it of the other religions; until she strings the pearls of the Christian religion upon the same thread of truth and makes the recognition of all reach around the world and touch the hearts of all.

You see that her work today is just a continuation of a different part of the same work. You cannot expect a person, even on the physical plane, to go on day after day, year after year, repeating the same thing. If he has a philosophy he must emphasize those aspects which will meet the needs of the day; for it is not a philosophy if it cannot fit all times and all conditions of life. If you send a child to school and he is taught the multiplication table and learns it perfectly, and then learns somethung else and finally a proffesion, would you say: "This cannot be the same child, for this knowledge is not what he was taught in the grammar school, and he is now quite different! " Do you not see Theosophists today who use no more common sense than this?

When the cycle of my work is closed; when this 1975 they talk so much about, comes, then there will be a new Agent or Messenger from the Lodge. Who will this new Messenger be? Ah, my children, that we must leave. It will be One whose understanding is opened, one who has wisdom, who has love and sympathy, who can touch the hearts and unfold the Heart Doctrine. His work will be a different work from mine, but a continuation of it. But in the meantime you can all help to spread the real Theosophy, both the body structure and the heart. You can thus help to redeem the work that is attributed to Mme. Blavatsky when on Earth; can be setting it right, by making people understand that while she was a human being, full of faults and failings, yet she was a chosen Messenger of the Lodge. She was also an immortal Spirit and a divinely appointed Teacher whose work is not taken from her because she laid down the human body of flesh; for *she is still working and will still work and never lay down her work*, until she has not merely one agent on Earth, but many, who will catch the rhythm of the true Teachings and will give but Theosophy from the heart side.

Why has the Society failed to touch the lives and hearts of its followers as it should? Because they cut out its heart and now are trying through magic to hold the atoms of the outer body together. Like all corpses, in spite of the mummy wrappings, the ritual and the mystic powers, the little atoms are gradually separating, and seeking to live their lives in peace and harmony elsewhere. Everything that is good in the old society—and there is much good— will be utilized. But there are still some devoted servants of the Lodge who are nevertheless so ignorant, so blinded, so deaf that they can look only backward, never forward. They see only that which was, never what now is, let alone what shall be. All that is good will manifest. Every teaching will come back renewed, *with its heart in it*. There is nothing that is hid that shall not be revealed, nothing buried that shall not be resurrected.

This is all I care to tell you. You can proclaim it at your discretion and let who will believe you. Let those who are blind be blind still, as the Bible tells us. And he that is deaf and lame and halt, let him be so still. For the "Kingdom of Heaven" cometh like a thief in the night. Did you ever stop to realize what this means? The night that the Scripture was alking about was the night of the world that we are passing through today; this great night of darkness and suffering and ignorance. Yet through the night the footsteps of the Angel messengers of the New Day can be heard. They are coming quietly, yet steadily and persistently. They come like a thief in the night, because they are stealing from the old forms their life, that which was thought to be their exclusive foundation. And as they come to humanity they must steal away from the old forms their life, their force, and their supremacy. And the result at first is more inharmony. Yet it is but like a mighty wind that is stirring up the dead leaves.

Soon, ah, so soon, will come the Great Gardener, like a fire, and burn up the chaff. The fire will be the fire of the Law, the fire of conviction, the fire of might and power. It will not be perhaps an outer fire—although that too, may manifest because the outer fire destroys—but the purifying inner fire, the fire of the heart, of the life, of the words. That is the fire that burns for ever and ever; that destroys ultimately all chaff and prepares the soil for new growth. This is all I have for you tonight. With my great love I bid you adieu.

Chapter XII

PHYSICAL PROOFS:
GENERAL SUBJECT

The physical proofs given in the following chapters place the subject of *conscious personal survival* beyond all argument. It is a physical fact scientifically proven, with physical evidence, and no longer dependent alone upon the reports of any mediums or even upon the record of any Scripture which relates the same facts such as the appearance of Moses and Elias to Jesus and His disciples on the Mount of Transfiguration, and the thirteen appearances of Jesus to His disciples elsewhere. The evidence can be duplicated by any sincere investigator who will take the trouble to set up the conditions necessary for successful experiments.

Persons who try to argue about the facts of survival are simply ignorant of the scientific facts repeatedly demonstrated by competent authorities. Literally they do not know what they are talking about. It is no longer a matter of belief but of fact.

Even before the development of Radar and the Atomic Bomb, no thoughtful scientist would say of any new discovery or idea; "It is impossible! It is against all the laws of science and nature." Much less would such scientists express a dogmatic opinion about a subject which they had not studied and personally investigated, any more than they would dare to express an adverse opinion as to the manufacture of the Atomic Bomb, without having had special training in nuclear, physics and atom splitting.

No matter how learned they may be on other subjects, they

should not allow themselves to express an opinion on such a technical matter as this without having been trained in the technique of this speciality. They only show their ignorance by doing so.

When such recognized scientific authorities as Alfred Russell Wallace, Sir William Crooks, Sir Arthur Conan Doyle, Professor Camille Flammarion, Professor F. W. H. Myers, and Sir William Barrett of England; Professors Charles Richet and Gustave Geley of France; Professors Cesar Lombroso and Ernesto Bozzano, and Dr. Joseph Lapponi, of Italy; Dr. A. Schrenck-Notzing, Dr. Franz Hartmann, and Dr. Johann Karl Jallner of Germany; Professor Harold Nielsson of Norway; Professor Alberto Brenes of Costa Rica; Professors James Hervey Hyslop, and Walter E. Prince of Boston; Professor William James and Dr. Crandon of Harvard; Professors McDougall and Joseph Banks Rhine of Duke; Professors Robert Hare, and Hilprecht, and Dr. Hays Agnew of the University of Pennsylvania; Robert J. Tillyard, Chief-Entomologist of the Commonwealth of Australia, and a host of others; when such great scientists, professors, and doctors, after careful investigation and experiment, pronounce survival a scientifically demonstrated fact, the opinion of lesser scientists who have not made special investigation into the subject are of little value.

SCIENTISTS TESTIMONIALS:

Sir Arthur Conan Doyle says, "I have never in my thirty years of experience, known one single scientific man who went thoroughly into this matter who did not end by accepting the spiritual solution."

Professor Lombroso for a long time ridiculed the claims of Psychic Research for survival after death, but when he was induced to investigate, he offered this handsome apology. "I am ashamed and grieved at having opposed the psychic facts. Genuine psychic phenomena are produced by intelligences totally independent of the parties present."

"I am absolutely convinced of the fact that those who once lived on earth, can and do communicate with us. It is hardly possible to convey to the inexperienced, an adequate idea of the strength and cumulative force of the evidence!" Sir William Barrett, F.R.S.

The famed Sir Oliver Lodge said, "I tell you we *do persist*. Communication is *possible*. I have proved that the people who communicate are who and what they say they are. The conclusion is, that survival is scientifically proved by scientific investigation."

"I am constrained to believe by the invincible logic of facts." Professor Raoul Pictet, University of Genoa.

Dr. Gustave Geley, of the Metapsychic Institute, Paris, states; "The facts necessitate the complete overthrow of the materialistic philosophy and conception of the Universe."

"When I remember that I branded as a fool that fearless investigator Crookes, because he had the courage to assert the reality of psychic phenomena, I am ashamed both of myself and others, and I cry from the very bottom of my heart, 'Father forgive! I have sinned against the Light.'" "Professor Ochorowicz, University of Warsaw.

A person may not believe that water is composed of two gases, oxygen and hydrogen in the proportions of H_2O, for any one can see that water is a liquid. But the fact of its being composed of two gases is not open to argument. It is simply a question of how familiar one is with the laws of chemistry. Likewise, anyone who argues against the truth of survival, simply exposes his ignorance of the facts discovered through scientific research.

It makes no difference—except to yourself—whether you believe in it or not. It is a fact in Nature whether you are familiar with it or not.

Scientific, well proven assurance of personal survival, is one of the greatest boons that humanity can receive. In the face of the stark tragedies of war, famine and pestilence, what a blessing it is to be positively assured that personal survival is beyond doubt.

Modern scientific investigation into this subject does not have to depend on the imperfect reports of our senses, which are subject to illusions, but relies largely on reports of scientific instruments, which are not subject to psychological reactions or illusions.

Even if these psychic phenomena are super-physical, they are not supernatural, hence should not be treated either as "spooky'" or to be worshipped as Divine. They are just natural phenomena, of a super-physical causation, and some day they will be so familiar to sincere students, as to cause no astonishment. They will seem as commonplace and taken for granted as the former mystery of radio, television and radar.

TYPES OF PHYSICAL PROOFS:

As we have said before, the whole subject of personal survival and every type of physical proof, has been thoroughly investigated by trained investigators, in laboratories equipped with special scientific instruments, and with light enough to see everything in the room, and with every precaution taken to prevent fraud. To obtain best results, special conditions have to be established, and special tecqniques have to be used, just as they do for any other scientific investigation. As the result of years of such investigation, and thousand of tests which confirm one another, some *types of physical proofs* of personal survival have been obtained, and repeatedly verified by independent investigators in widely separated countries.

Some of these types of physical proofs we will study in the following pages.

Chapter XIII

SPIRIT PHOTOGRAPHS
AND SKOTOGRAPHS

Proofs of identity depend on many factors. Primarily these are based on certain characteristics which remain in evidence, despite changes in appearance. Probably no one evidence would constitute absolute proof of identity, at least not for everyone, for only by the accumulation of several types of evidence, can positive proof be established. While photographs are generally accepted as certainty, their variability prevents them from being absolute proof. Not only does the photographer present to us pictures of several different poses for our selection, each one varying in appearance sometimes markedly, but we ourselves change in appearance, sometimes more, sometimes less, from month to month, and from year to year. Often this change is quite marked, but in general our characteristics are sufficiently definite for photographs to be accepted as evidence of identity.

Spirit Photographs:

Therefore, while spirit photographs are not considered to be *absolute proof* of identity, they may well be considered as a great contribution to the mass of proof that is being accumulated to prove personal survival and direct communication with those of the spirit world.

There are still some unenlightened people who claim that spirit photography cannot *be*, since, they say, "that which is invisible cannot be photographed." But science has proven

PLATE V—Sir Arthur, taken by son Dennis.

PLATE VI—Picture before the Cenotaph in London, Armistice Day.

that there are many substances,—chemicals and gases—that, while not visible to the naked eye, are sufficiently tangible to produce an image on the photographic plate. And so in the same way spirit photography can be produced.

There are two methods of producing spirit photography. In one of these the spirit is directly before the camera, partially materialized. In all spirit photography the same unchanging characteristics which give evidence of identity when photos are taken under test conditions of those who have long departed from this Earth, are good evidence of their identity, in the strictest sense.

In the first method of producing spirit photographs, there must be present one or more persons who have the ability to exude from their bodies enough etheric matter, *ectoplasm*, for the deceased ones who wished to be photographed to use to materialize their astral bodies to a density sufficient to affect the photographic plate or film, even though not dense enough to be visible to the naked eye.

SOME SPIRIT PHOTOGRAPHS:

Thousands of photographs have been taken with ordinary cameras with plates sealed in a package by the dealers at the time of purchase, and unopened until placed in the cameras by chosen judges. Lady Conan Doyle sent the writer spirit pictures of Sir Arthur Conan Doyle taken in her own home by her son Dennis with his own camera and plates two years after Sir Arthur's graduation from Earth life. This picture we produce herein.

We have seen hundreds of similar identified photographs taken under test conditions which definitely rule out all chance of fraud or trick photography.

One of the most spectacular and convincing of such photographs we have ever seen, and which we also produce herein, was one taken several years ago out-of-doors at the Cenotaph in Whitehall, London, on Armistice Day. At a certain spot in front of the Cenotaph, a group of some 200 Spiritualists were kneeling in prayer. When the plate was developed, there was revealed a cloud of ectoplasm over the group. In this cloud were found the pictures of faces of more than 60 deceased British soldiers, most of whose faces were identified later. The cloud of ectoplasm was so dense that it obscured most of the Cenotaph and some of the branches of the nearby trees. The remarkable thing about this picture is that it was taken out-of-doors in broad daylight in the presence of thousands of spectators where any fraud was impossible.

SKOTOGRAPHS:

As we have said before there are two methods of producing spirit photography and the second of these is called skotography. Skotographs are pictures impressed upon the photographic plate or film in complete darkness and without the use of the camera or any known kind of light — infra-red or otherwise — except the inherent radiant light of the spirit world. Thus no camera is required.

A good account of this rare type of mediumship is the experience of the Rev. J. T. Wills, D.D., Pastor of the Franklin Street Presbyterian Church of San Francisco. In 1903 he investigated the claims of Dr. W. J. Pierce, a business man of the highest integrity, who claimed to have taken pictures without a camera, in connection with the mediumship of Mr. Edward Wyllie. On the day appointed for the test Rev. Wills bought a package of plates at a photo supply store, and carried them in his pocket to the Doctor's office where he was to meet the medium. The Doctor, who was an amateur photographer, had a dark room and all the equipment for development. The two entered the dark room which was lighted by the usual orange light used by photographers. In his account of the experiment he says:

"I took the plates out of my pocket, and took one plate out of the package. After marking it on one corner, I took it by the corners toward me and held it out to the medium who, placing his hands one on top and the other underneath, held the plate between his palms. I continued to hold the plate by its corners and never let go of it for an instant. To my surprise I heard three distinct taps upon the plate; the medium removed his hands and I put the plate at once into the developer and developed it myself, *no one but myself touching it for an instant*. Neither was the plate out of my possession for one second from the time I bought it until I had it fully developed. To my astonishment there was the face of a lady on it, and so plain that it was recognized by my daughter as the likeness of a lady who was never in California, and who died in England several years ago. . . . In the course of about fifteen minutes we had four tests, and with four distinct and different faces with the same medium, and in the same manner. Then I felt compelled to acknowledge that by a force not visible to me, this work had been done." [1]

The following photograph is the one taken by the Rev. J. T. Wills, D.D. and described above.

The following inscription on the back of the photograph below, was written by Dr. Pierce;

"Obtained in London England, Oct. 8th, 1903, under strictly test conditions, within a box holding six sensitized plates; no camera used. The plates were purchased, developed and fixed by me, the medium doing nothing except to hold the unopened box between his hands for about two minutes, prior to the developing." [2]

Geoffrey O'Hara, composer of *There Is No Death*, gives a description of the very rigid scientific tests, to which this picture above was put to prove its authenticity, in *The Psychic Observer*, Jan. 10th, 1945.

In this psychic photograph, or skotograph, the extra of Will Rogers,—center—is a most positive proof of survival. This picture was verified as evidential by Congressman Adolph J. Sabath. A fairly distinct picture, that bears a remarkable resemblance to the late Sir Oliver Lodge, can be

---

[1] *The Widow's Mite*, Funk, 463-5.
[2] *The Widow's Mite*, Funk, 475.

seen upper center. The spirit extra to the right center has been definitely claimed as that of Lon Chaney.[3]

This skotograph of flowers was precipitated for the author under strictly tested and scientific conditions.

Although the subject is consistently avoided by his biographers, there is ample documentary evidence to show that President Lincoln was an ardent Spiritualist. He not only attended Séances of the celebrated medium Mrs. L. . . . But even had materializing séances held in the White House, with the child medium Nettie Colburn.

The following psychic photograph of Abraham Lincoln, obtained in 1925, through the mediumship of Craig and George Falconer, noted English mediums, has been published numerous times in London Spiritualistic Journals. It is recognized as probably the most outstanding spirit photograph of Lincoln on record and was obtained under strict test conditions.

THE MASTER JESUS:

Of course there were no pictures of the Master Jesus made during his Earth-life. All the pictures now in existence are but the conceptions of the various artists. This picture was precipitated for the author directly from the invisible. The discarnate artist stated that the radiance of the Master was so glorious that it almost blinded him.

This sketch was the best he could do under the circumstances. When it was finished he precipitated it into the physical for our use. The face is sensitive and kind, without being effeminate; strong, positive and masculine without being stern.

---

[3] For further details see *Psychic Observer*, Sept. 10th, 1944.
Note — Unless otherwise stated these psychic photographs and skotographs are used through the courtesy of the *Psychic Observer*.

CHAPTER XIV

HANDWRITING, PSYCHOGRAPHS AND SIGNATURES

Our handwriting although it varies from year to year, still retains and exhibits certain characteristics which make it easily recognizable as being ours. This is especially true of our signature. Even when we try to disguise our handwriting, experts can detect the attempt and recognize the writer. But these variations do not prevent bank officials from accepting the slightly varying signatures to our checks. Consequently, when our departed loved ones send us messages, either through controlled, automatic writing of someone living on Earth, or by messages in their own characteristic handwriting, which are phenomenally precipitated intact from the astral, the writing is so characteristic of the departed ones, as to be easily recognized by anyone familiar with their handwriting. This is another good evidence of their presence and identity, even though it may not be absolute proof to the severe critic.

PSYCHOGRAPHS:

We have spoken above of messages precipitated direct and intact from the astral by discarnate spirits. These messages are called psychographs and the method of receiving them is called psychography. Psychographs are obtained without human contact, and are shown by rigid tests to be the work of discarnate entities.

PRECIPITATED WRITING:

This writing was originally called "slate writing" as it was usally precipitated on the dark space between two slates or on cards placed there. The way this is accomplished is as follows: The inquiring sitter writes out the desired questions, addressed to his departed loved ones. These are then laced in a sealed envelope, so that the medium can have no knowledge of either the questions or the names of the persons addressed. The sealed envelope is then placed outside on top of the slates. The spirit-guide transmits the messages telepathically to the loved ones so addressed, and collects their replies.

The departed ones addressed write out their answers to the questions asked by the sitter, and then the guide, again using the psychic forces of the medium, precipitates the writing either on the slates or on the cards placed between the slates.

In some instances the materialized hand of the spirit visitor is able to do the writing on paper and with a real pencil.

While trying to solve an old mystery of her brother's recorded death in the first World War, Sylvia Barbanell, a noted author and investigator of psychic phenomena, proved beyond a doubt that she received a direct message from the brother who *had gone over*. At a séance he asked for a pencil and paper and with his materialized hand, he wrote her a letter, clearing up the mystery of his death. On comparing this letter with the others he had written, the writing was found to be identical, and even the manner of finishing his letter and signing his name was beyond doubt. The medium who was conducting the séance at the time had never seen the boy's handwriting and Miss Barbanell had none of his letters with her at the time.[1]

The method of spirit-writing on slates seems not to be as yet fully comprehended probably because earth people are not sufficiently advanced in scientific knowledge, as known

[1] For further details see, *When Your Animal Dies*, Barbanell, 24.

PLATE VII—Sir Arthur Conan Doyle surrounded by his spirit friends.

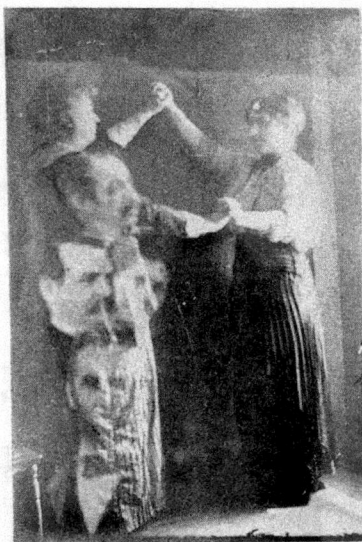

PLATE VIII—Abraham Lincoln, with Ralph Waldo Emerson, Edward Everett Hale and Grover Cleveland.

PLATE IX—Child Medium Lily, and others from the spirit-world.

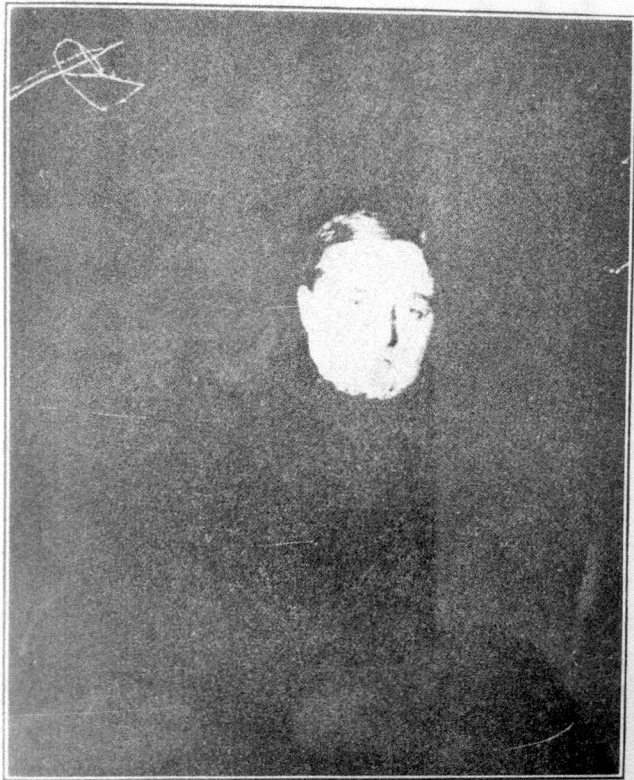

PLATE X—Spirit photograph of Lady's head.

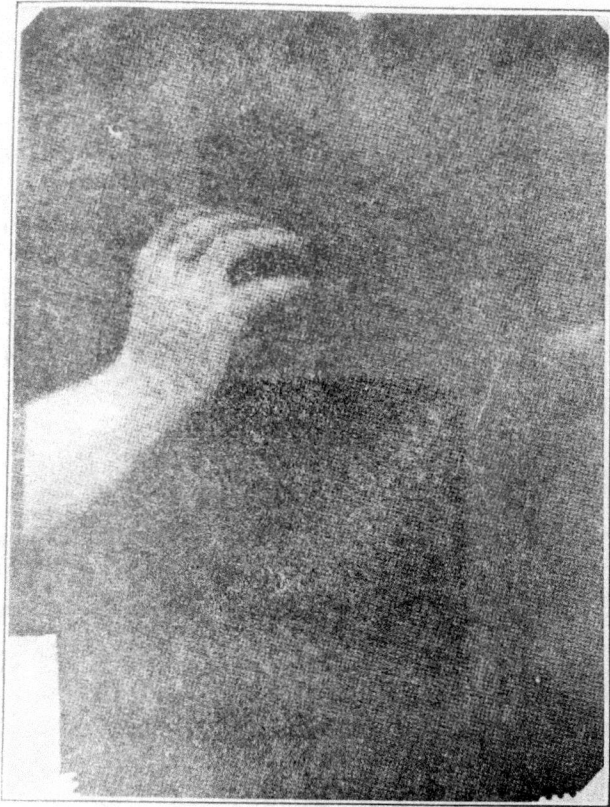

PLATE XI—Spirit picture of hand.

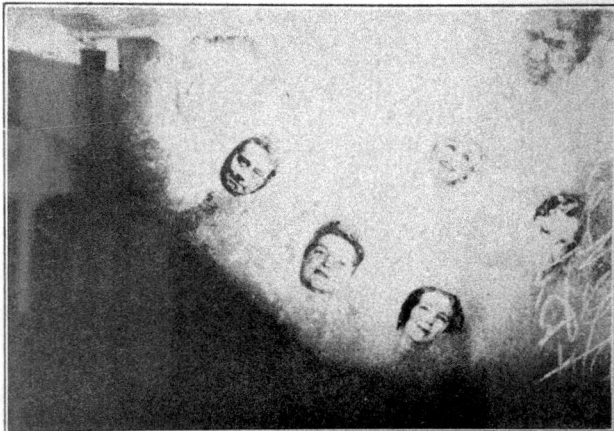

PLATE XII—Spirit photograph of Wendell Willkie and Al Smith.

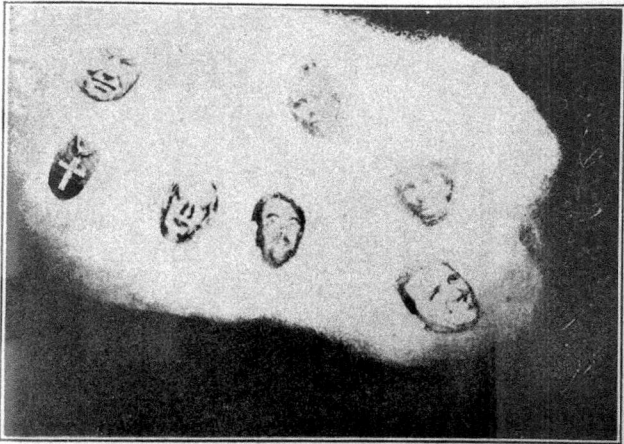

PLATE XIII—Spirit picture of Willkie, Geofrey O'Hara and others.

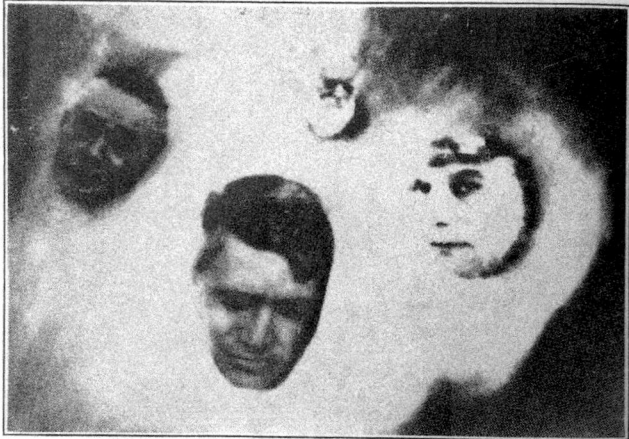

PLATE XIV—Will Rogers, Lon Chaney and others.

PLATE XV—Precipitated picture of flowers.

PLATE XVI—Head of Lincoln.

PLATE XVII—The Master Jesus.

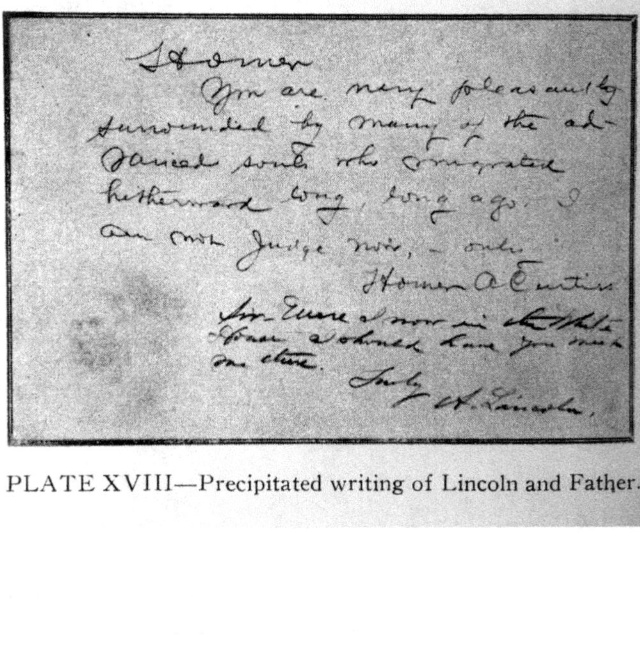

Homer

You are very pleasantly surrounded by many of the advanced souls who emigrated hitherward long, long ago. I am not Judge now, — only

Homer A Curtiss

[illegible] I [illegible] in the White House [illegible] have you [illegible] one there.

Truly

A. Lincoln.

PLATE XVIII—Precipitated writing of Lincoln and Father.

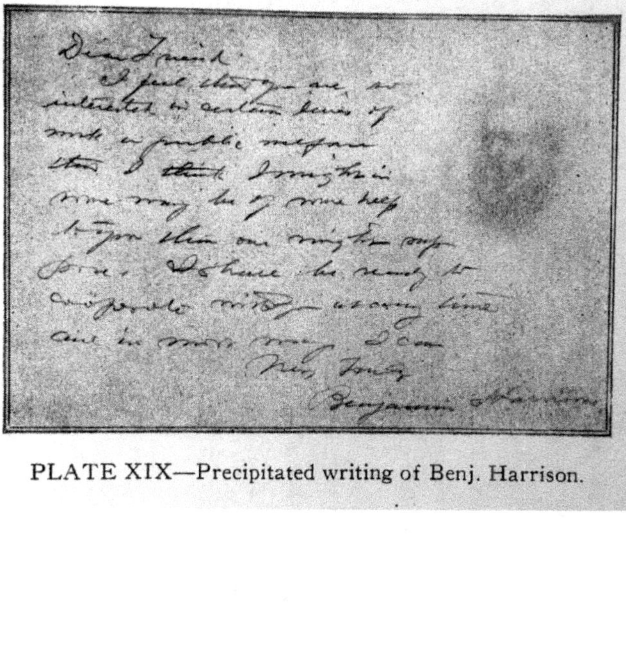
Dear Friend:
I feel that you are so interested in certain lines of work in public welfare that I think I might in some way be of some help to you other than one might suppose. I shall be ready to cooperate with you at any time and in most ways. I am
Very truly
Benjamin Harrison

PLATE XIX—Precipitated writing of Benj. Harrison.

"Crowned with coral blooms on flying backs reposing
Thy loved-ones wait thee; O, one fond embrace
One with look from eyes their love disclosing
Shall compensate thee for this mortal race
And every sorrow from thy heart efface."

We are not lost to our friends by transition; for we do visit them from our higher realm of being. You do not see us with your slow vibrating physical eye, for the swift wave motion of the spirit causes it to be lost to your mortal sight. It is to be hoped that someday the mortal vision may be quickened, and then these we shall be, this infinitely, we shall be together in the better land. But we are to be up getting for those left behind, and so you this calm, sabbath spring morning, I am coming again.

Dear Mother
Sarah D Curtis

I am not able to write a long letter this time. I am trusting and need to you my continued life and nearness and gathering on heartily yours.

PLATE IV. ... reading of "mother" and "Annie."

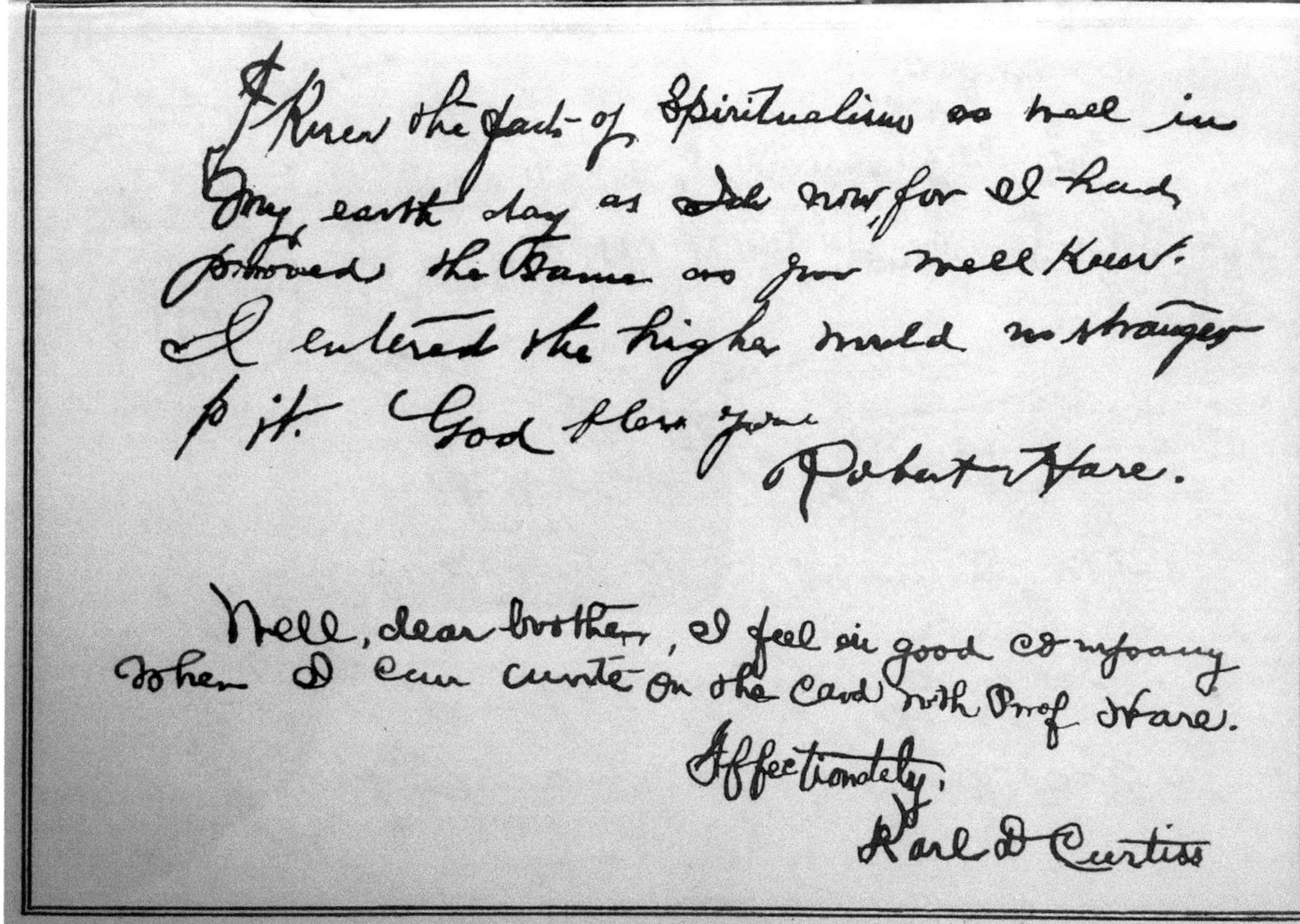

No think required. Should keep a

to get a bone out of his throat.

Can't. Certainly or a Human Being.

Staff Press Agent.

The India Message and ready at present. We have

to look for the proper direction of Contradiction etc.

Karl.

by the spirits to understand the process. Usually a small bit of pencil is placed between the slates, but it would seem that the spirits do not always have to use this. A group of mediums, "sitting" without any outsiders in the meeting, once requested the spirits to write on the slates with a bright orange color, taken from a ribbon worn by one of the mediums. The color of the writing on the slates, when compared with that of the ribbon, matched exactly.[1]

It has been the author's privilege to have received a number of messages from his father, mother, brothers and sister; also from former Professors of the University of Pennsylvania, Former Presidents Lincoln, Benjamin Harrison and other distinguished personages have also written us messages.

In each case the writing was characteristic of the communicator as the signatures were verified by comparisons with those left behind at their passing. On one occasion President Lincoln precipitated a picture of himself with the message as did Benjamin Harrison.

The following are some of the psychographs we have mentioned above. These messages definitely refute the claim of some skeptics that spirit messages are of a trivial nature, give little information, and are of low intellectual content.

These psychographs were materialized by Pierre L. O. A. Keeler, at Cascadoga, Fla., Easter morning, March 27th, & Easter Monday March 28th, 1932 for F. Homer Curtiss.

The author did not recognize the signature of "Annie," but when this message was thrown on the screen at a meeting, a lady in the audience recognized the writing and signature as belonging to a friend who had passed over to the spirit world some time before.

Professor Hare was formerly Professor of Chemistry at the University of Pennsylvania, and had been interested in the facts of Spiritualism for some time before his passing.

Dr. Agnew was formerly Professor of Surgery at the

---

[1] For further details see *Evidential Slate Writing*, Washburn, *The Direct Voice*, Sept, 1930.

University of Pennsylvania where Dr. Curtiss took his Medical Degree many years later.

Dr. Curtiss was attending a dinner in Florida, when one of the guests swallowed a bone which lodged so far down in the trachea that all ordinary efforts to remove it failed and he was in grave danger of choking to death. During the interim while a surgeon was being sought. Dr. Curtiss received a message from Dr. Agnew from the other side to administer a tremendous blow at a certain spot on the man's back. He jumped from his chair and followed the instructions, with a resounding whack. The bone flew out on the floor. The above psychographic message was received psychographically from Dr. Agnew in reply to Dr. Curtiss' sincere thanks.

CHAPTER XV

MATERIALIZATION

Materialization of form, to such an extent as to be seen and felt by human beings, is another contributing evidence of personal survival, after so-called death. This is accomplished by the departed one's drawing from the body of the materializing medium, and from that of the audience, enough of their etheric material or "ectoplasm," to clothe himself, and make his astral body dense enough to be seen in the dark faintly glowing with an inner radiant light.

ECTOPLASM:

This ectoplasm is the substance of the etheric body of the medium, or others in the séance room, which is the duplicate of the physical body, and into the meshes of which the substance of the dense body is materialized.

Just as certain persons are born with special talents for music, art, song, mathematics or other abilities, so certain persons are born with the ability to exude some of their etheric substance, or ectoplasm, through their orifices, usually the mouth and nose. Sometimes this emerges only as a thin vapor, but may be condensed into a liquid or even a solid on sufficient contact with the air. Since this substance is semi-physical in its vaporous condition it is used by the discarnate spirits and incorporated into their astral bodies to make them sufficiently dense to be seen or photographed, or to produce the higher, lighter types of physical phenomena. From its liquid state it can be condensed into rigid rods, or it can be moulded into other forms, which are capable of lifting or sustaining considerable weight, or producing other phenomena which require the application of great force.

We have personally felt this condensed ectoplasm, and its touch resembles that of a jelly, which tends to dissolve under the living hand, and usually melts away rapidly in the presence of light, as it is withdrawn into the body of the medium.

Repercussion:

Since the ectoplasm of the etheric body is the substance of the model on which the physical body is built, if it is injured in any way while it is exuded from the medium's body,—such as by bruising, scratching, or cutting, when it is withdrawn again into the body of the medium, the damage will be reproduced in the flesh, manifesting as a bruise, scratch, or even a bleeding cut. This phenomena is called repercussion. Therefore it is very dangerous to the welfare of the medium, for anyone to touch the ectoplasm or materialized form without the permission of the controlling guide. If the astral cord connecting the medium with the materialized form is severed and the ectoplasm is thus prevented from returning into the physical body, it may result in the death of that body. Those who attend materializing séances should understand this, and rigidly adhere to the rules laid down as to the touching of any materialized forms or articles, or they will be responsible for any unhappy results.

Even the sudden unauthorized turning on of the light may dissolve the ectoplasm so quickly, that it will produce a great shock to the medium from which it will require weeks to recover. Since ectoplasm is usually soluble in light, such materializations have to be produced in the dark, or under a faint ruby light.

Because they are more often produced in the dark, these phenomena are most often imitated or "faked," but this can be detected by photographing materialized figures, with infra-

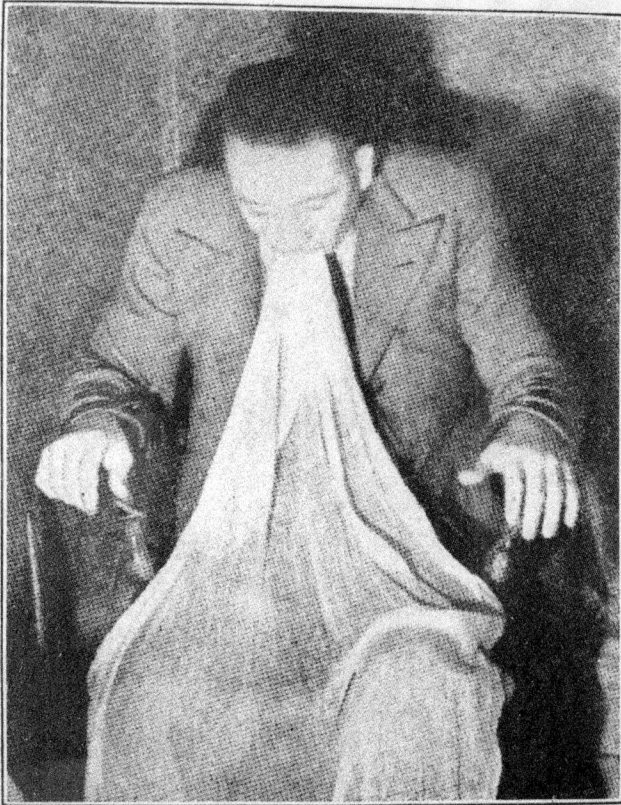

PLATE XXIII—Ectoplasm. Over five yards long.

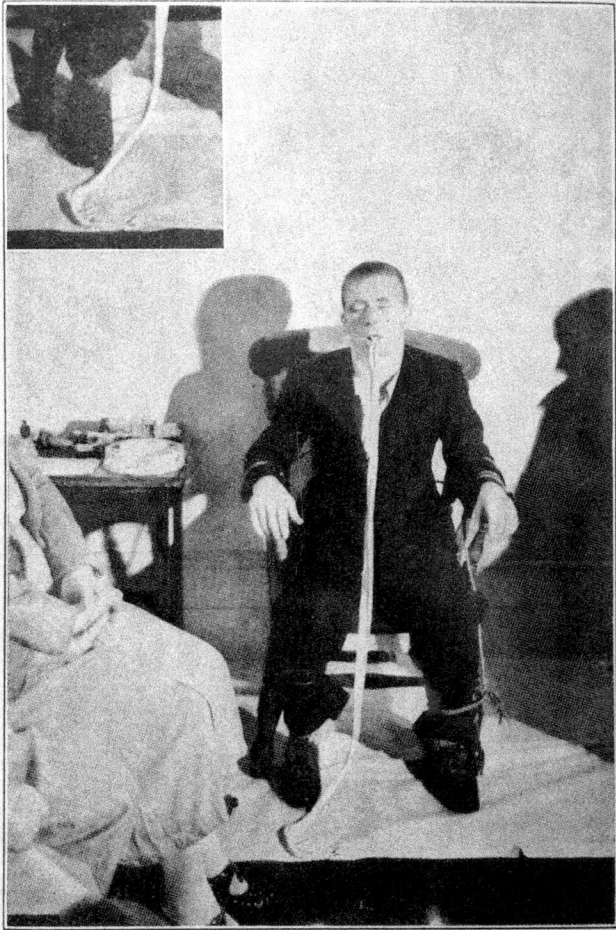

PLATE XXIV—Ectoplasmic arm. Note grippers at the end of arm for clasping objects. Also orifice above the grippers.

red rays which, as we explained above, can take pictures in the dark.

MATERIALIZATION IN THE LIGHT:

There are certain exceptions to this general law of materializing in the dark, however, for some mediums have the extraordinary ability to produce materialization in the daylight.

The most astonishing exception we have found recorded, is that of the noted English medium, William Englinton. On one occasion while he lay in a trance on a bench out-of-doors in the garden, he materialized several human forms, taller than himself. One of them was so powerful that it lifted the hat off the head of a spectator, put it on its own head, walked a distance of more than sixty feet from the entranced medium, returned, gave the hat back to its owner, shook hands with him and then melted back into the body of the medium. This was aptly testified to and verified by those present.

During our years of personal investigation, among the hundreds of materialized figures we have seen, all of which were recognized by relatives or friends, our mother once fully materialized, and walked the entire length of a large faintly lighted living-room in full view of some twenty persons. She came up to us, patted us on the cheek and said in a loud whisper, "Bless you, my son." Other members of our family have materialized since in the same way.

On one of the author's visits to "Margery," he was shown three large rings, each of a different kind of wood, but each interlaced with the other two. At the time they were shown to him, they had to be shown under a ruby light as they were still considered to be "green"; that is, they had not been materialized long enough to be sufficiently solid to withstand daylight without dissolving. Later, these rings were submitted to photomicrographic and other laboratory tests to discover if they had been cut in two in any way to interlace them, and then cemented together again. No such transverse joint could be found. This again proves that, supenormally, one form of matter can interpenetrate and pass through another.

During a period of three years. Sir William Crookes', in experiments with the medium Florence Cook, frequently witnessed the full sized figure of Katie King, who was six inches taller than the medium, in a somewhat dim light. Katie at times walked about the room for two hours, conversing in a distinctly audible voice. The medium habitually wore earings while the materialized figure did not. Her form was so solid that she was able to grant the request of Sir William that he might hold her in his arms, where he felt her living body. She was frequently photographed, at one time with five cameras,—including a stereoscopic camera,—focused on her figure at the same time. At each séance, at least three exposures of each camera were given.

It was a common thing for the spectators to see both Katie King and the medium together in the full glare of the electric light. The pulse of Katie beat steadily at seventy-five, while that of Miss Cook was going at the rate of ninety. This shows that Katie's astral heart was beating as regularly as it did in physical life.[1]

Materialized forms have been heard to breathe heavily, and on certain occasions the breath was breathed through a tube into *baryta* water, to detect the presence of carbon dioxide. A bubbling was heard and the dioxide was proved to be present, showing that physiological metabolic changes were taking place in the body of the spirit visitor.

This is positive proof that the form was densely materialized, that it was performing all the physiological functions of normal respiration—namely, breathing in oxygen and breathing out carbonic acid gas—as any other living human being must necessarily do.

Mediums have been known to lose as much as sixty pounds while the figures are materialized. In Colonel Alcott's ex-

---

[1] See *One Hundred Cases of Survival After Death*, Baird, 209.

periments, at the Eddy's at Chittenden, he had various materialized forms step on a platform scales, on which the weights were recorded, or measured, and they were found to vary from one hundred and thirty-two to one hundred and sixty pounds.[2]

On one occasion materialized hands pulled a spring scale out to the limit of measurement, which was fifty pounds. And as we have said before, materialized figures have extraordinary strength. In a number of instances the materialized figure was able to pick up the entranced medium in his arms and carry her all around the room for the sitters to see.

In another instance, the materialized form was able to answer the telephone and have her voice recognized by the caller.

As the materialized figure moves around the room, everyone is able to see it since it is illumined by its own inner radiance.

In her book, *Ghosts I Have Seen*, Violet Tweedale, a writer of note and a person of integrity, and impeccable character, tells of a remarkable demonstration of materialization on one of her visits to Mme. Blavatsky in London. She says. "On another occasion when I was alone with Madame Blavatsky, she suddenly broke off our conversation by lapsing into another language, which I supposed to be Hindustani. She appeared to be addressing someone else, and on looking over my shoulder, I saw that we were no longer alone. A man stood in the middle of the room. I was sure he had not entered by the door, window or chimney, and as I looked at him in astonishment, he salaamed to Mme. Blavatsky, and replied to her in the same language in which she had addressed him."

The picture below is one of the materialized form and particularly the *hands*, of Archbishop Nathan Soderblom of Sweden, given to his medium the Swedish Pastor Martin Liljeblad. The archbishop had previously written a theolog-

---

[2] *Peoples from the Other Worlds*, Olcott, 256-57.

ical treatise, through the automatic writing of Liljeblad. This photograph was recognized by many persons
who knew him well, as an authentic one of the "dead"
archbishop.

Liljeblad also published a book of hymns, given to him
through automatic writing from the Danish Hymn writer
Bishop Kingo, who had passed on many years ago. Because
he could not find any suitable tunes for his hymns, he was
helped by other spirits to compose the music for some of
the hymns which he had received through mediumship.

PLATE XXV—Materialized form and hands of Archbishop Nathan Soderblom.

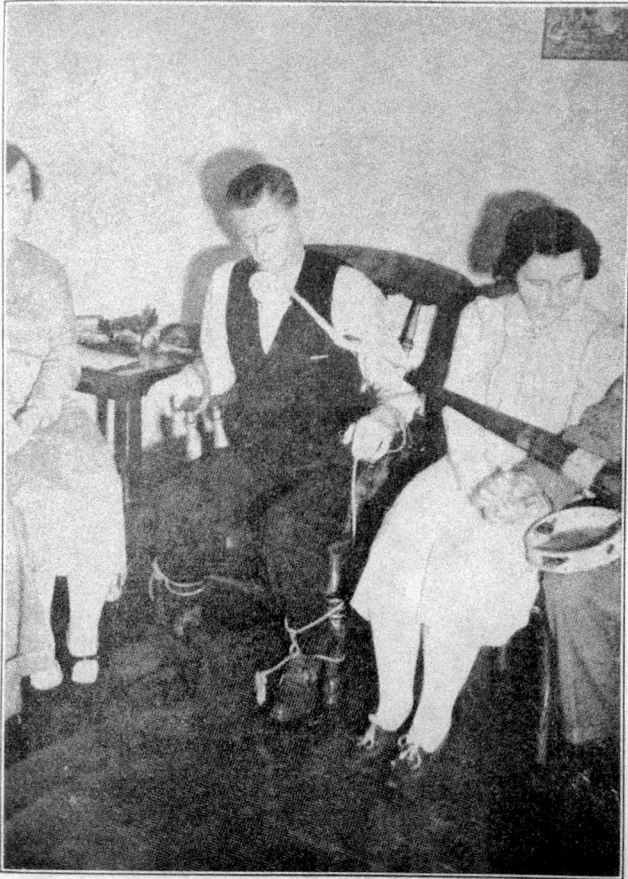

PLATE XXVI—Ectoplasmic voice box, used by spirit visitors in speaking directly to the sitters.

PLATE XXVII—The trumpets are connected by two ectoplasmic arms, one from the mouth and the other from the solar plexus.

Chapter XVI

DIRECT VOICE

Another physical proof of personal survival is the voices of the departed coming through to those on this earthplane, and being recognized as such by them. The direct voice of a loved one can be heard only to the extent that he can materialize his larynx and vocal cords by using the ectoplasm of the medium. This takes considerable training and practice, and therefore at first only whispers can be produced. In this case a trumpet or megaphone can be used and later when the voice box is fully materialized, the characteristic tones of the speaker can be easily recognized and identified. To save expenditure of force, only the larynx of the medium needs to be materialized, as shown in the pictures following, taken with infra-red light.

TRUMPETS:

When a trumpet is used it is usually levitated in the air by spirit power and thus can float to any person in the room, as shown also in the pictures. The trumpet is often found near the ceiling, out of human reach.

Bands of luminous tape are frequently placed around each end of the trumpet, so that its movements can be seen by all present.

DIRECT VOICE:

Tones of the voice and the timbre of its vibrations are so characteristic that they are easily recognized in general.

When the voice of the departed is recorded on a phonograph disk, it may be analyzed scientifically and proved to be identical with similar disks recorded by that one before transition.

DIRECT VOICE PHENOMENA:

The following examples of direct voice are quoted by a writer on this subject: —

"At a sitting with the Countess Tyong Ceitiongham, a voice addressed her in Chinese, in which language a conversation was carried on between them for a short time. After the sitting the Countess stated that there were at least twenty dialects in Chinese, each of which might have been used. The voice, in speaking to her used two dialects mixed in a way in which no European—even if he were able to speak Chinese—could do. *One of the dialects was that in which her father used to speak to her when she was a child, and the other, one which they used in talking together after she had grown up.*"[1]

The following incident is quoted because the author [while living in Los Angeles] knew Dr. Peebles personally as a man of great integrity of purpose:

"A voice claiming to be Dr. Peebles spoke to Dr. Abraham Wallace. 'You remember that there was a banquet held in my honor, when the empty chair was left for me? I appreciated it very much; I enjoyed the gathering.'

"Afterwards Dr. Wallace explained that a banquet had been held in honor of the 100th birthday of Dr. Peebles, who died just prior to it. Nevertheless the banquet was held with the empty chair at the table in appreciation of Dr. Peebles. This incident was accepted as evidential by Dr. Wallace, as no one in the room knew of this happening but himself."[2]

In an experiment with Margery Crandon, the investigator placed a sensitive microphone in a locked and sealed box,

---

[1] *Peoples from the Other Worlds*, Alcott.
[2] *Peoples from the Other Worlds*. Alcott.

impervious to any sound-producing waves. The microphone was connected with a loud speaker in a distant part of the house, and "Walter's" voice was produced from the loud speaker, with no sound audible in the séance room.

The following case of independent voice is a remarkable and authentic one. One of our students, Mrs. B., attended a séance for the first time, in an attitude of neither belief or disbelief, but with rather a willingness to be shown. The medium had been getting messages of a general nature, through a trumpet, for the sitters, when from the center of the group came a voice calling distinctly Mrs. B.'s full name, and in tones loud enough to be heard by anyone in the circle. She at once *recognized* the voice as belonging to a friend who had passed over a few years back, and she greeted her in return. So sure was she of the identification that she called out; "Oh! Hello C. . . ." using her first name, just as she had often greeted her, when they had met before death had separated them.

C. . . . then spoke of a matter which had been troubling her, and said she had tried numerous times to get in touch with her friend, in order to try to get the trouble straightened out. *No one on earth knew of this incident save these two* and they conversed about it for a few minutes. Mrs. B. explained that it had been taken care of satisfactorily, at the time of C's passing over, and that now she might be at rest about it. C thanked her, spoke of some mutual friends in the spirit world and on the earth-plane, said "Good-bye" very distinctly and then her voice faded out completely. This was a most remarkable demonstration of the *Direct Voice* phenomenon, because of the fact that the spirit visitor spoke without the aid of the trumpet, and that Mrs. B. . . . did not expect either a visitor or a message, and that the matter discussed was positively known to these two alone.

May we further state that none of the sitters nor the medium had met Mrs. B. . . . or her spirit friend, before the night of the séance. It was a clear and true case of *Inde-*

pendent Voice, and a very convincing proof of personal survival after death.

"A remarkable variety of voices were reproduced through the trumpet at a séance by Armand Wilson, at the Great Metropolitan Spiritualist Association. Singers from the other world included a contralto, a mezzo-soprano, sopranos, and tenors—and some of them remarkably good—.... A mezzo-soprano who said she was the mother f the medium was asked to sing a song composed for a tenor voice. After a laugh all around, a tenor voice obliged with an excellent rendering of the song." The speaking voices at this séance were also remarkably loud and clear."[3]

---

[3] *Psychic News*, Jan. 19th. 1946.

Chapter XVII

FINGER PRINTS AND
WAX GAUNTLETS

One of the most convincing proofs of personal survival is fingerprints. In all the courts throughout the world fingerprints are now accepted as indisputable physical proof that the person to whom they belong must have been actually present to make them. Since this is true, and as no two persons have the same identical fingerprints, spirit fingerprints are positive and convincing proof of personal survival.

As proof that no two persons have the same fingerprints, among the many millions of them on file at the headquarters of the F.B.I. in Washington, at Scotland Yard in London, at the Sureté in Paris, and elsewhere, there are no two alike. Since it is now universally accepted that no two persons, *living or dead*, have the same fingerprints, only the owner could have made them. Therefore, as we have said above, fingerprints are recognized as positive and irrefutable proof of the presence and identity of the one who makes them. Even though they are taken of one who is no longer living on this earth-plane, and can be proven to belong to that one, there is absolute proof that the person is *personally "alive"* in some other realm.

Scientific investigators have found many such prints made in soft wax by persons who have passed on from earth-life, several years previously. These prints have been compared by fingerprint experts, with those made by the same persons while they were on Earth, and the two have been declared identical. This is *positive physical proof* that the owners must have materialized their fingers sufficiently solidly to have made the imprint on the wax.[1]

When such prints are made by the departed in melted wax, and after comparison with those made while still living they are proven identical, this constitutes, not merely evidence, but positive proof of that one's presence in a body which is an exact duplicate of the physical body, down to the minutest detail.

EXAMPLES:

Thumbprints of Charles S. Hill procured after death and under strict conditions of control.

The thumbprint on the left, was taken in 1928 before his death. That on the right was taken in 1930 after he had been in the spirit world over a year.

In another experiment with "Margery," William H. Button, then president of the American S.P.R., obtained a thumbprint in wax, inside a heavily locked box, which could not be opened without the facts becoming immediately apparent.[2]

WAX MOULDS:

There is probably no physical proof of personal survival more positive, convincing or indisputable, than wax moulds made from hands or feet, of discarnate beings. To produce this phenomena, large vases containing melted paraffin are placed before the materializing medium, whose hands are held by the judges, or otherwise so firmly secured that there is no possibility of their being moved. During the séance materialized arms, hands or fists, are dipped into the paraffin several times, until a thick coating is produced. This is allowed to harden, and then the materialized form is dematerialized, leaving a hollow gauntlet of hard wax. This is then filled with plaster of Paris, which makes a perfect cast of the limb or other object which was dematerialized. This is

---

[1] See *Journal of the American Society for Psychical Research.*
[2] *Journal of American Society for Psychical Research, January* 1934.

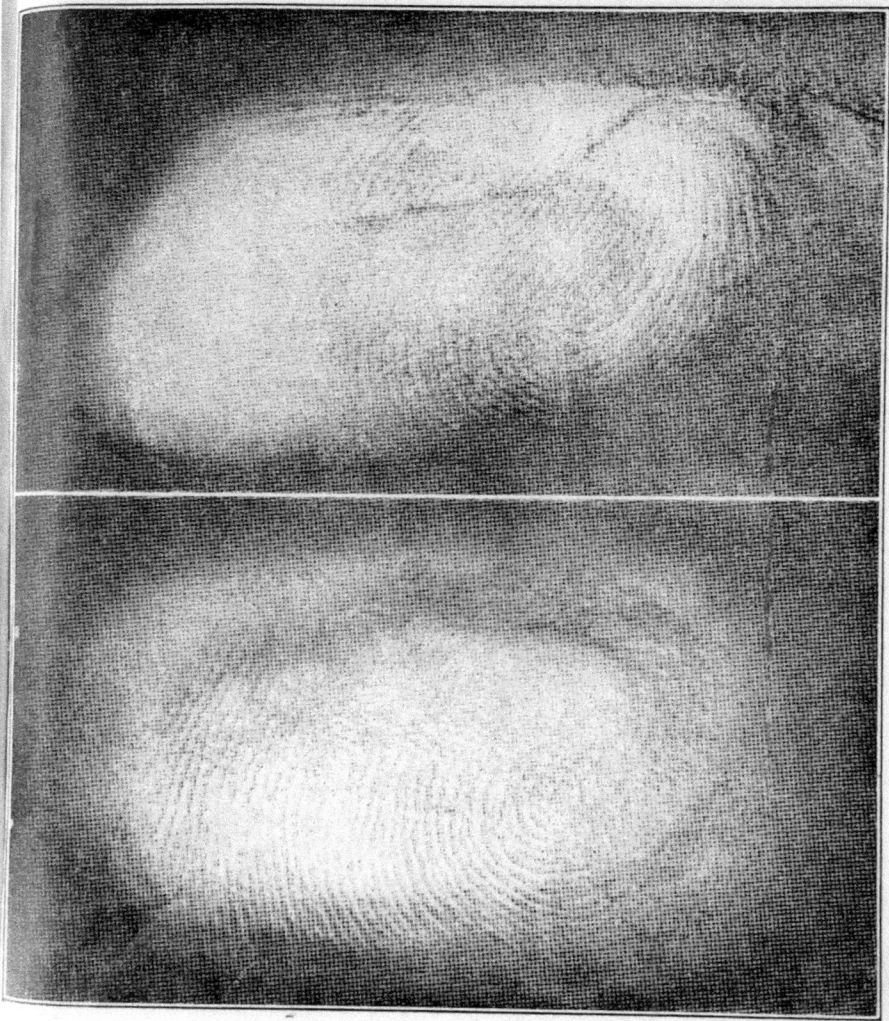

PLATE XXVIII—Fingerprints of Chas. Hill.

such an accurate reproduction tbat it shows the texture of the skin, location of creases, blood-vessels and disposition of the hair. In some cases it reveals scars, deformities or other special characteristics, which positively identify the deceased spirit who had materialized.

In the Spiritist Headquarters in Paris, there is a collection of famous psychic moulds, made by means of paraffin. These were obtained in the usual manner by placing a vessel of warm paraffin near the sitters, and the materialized forms were requested to thrust a hand or foot into the liquid, which was then allowed to cool. The mould thus made was then filled with plaster in the usual way and the paraffin removed. The moulds are of great variety, some of delicate female hands, some of large strong male hands while others are of children, or very small adult hands. These moulds were made under the mediumship of Kulaski, and conditions were such as to preclude the possibility of fraud.[1]

Since these plaster moulds of the hand, arm or other parts of the body, produced from wax gauntlets, *reproduce the identifiable characteristics of the size, shape, deformities, scars or other details of the departed one's limbs*, and since it would be impossible to duplicate such moulds in any other way, they may be regarded as such strong evidence of personal survival as to be proof to any reasonable mind.

This phenomenon is also positive proof of both materialization and dematerialization, first because the cast differs markedly from the hands and arms of the medium and secondly, if there is no dematerialization there would be no possible way by which the hand or closed fist could be withdrawn through the narrow portion of the wrist of the mould. The most skilled human moulders are unable to produce similar moulds without making them in halves, and afterwards uniting them. This is one more physical proof which defies any other explanation than personal survival of the deceased person in a materialized body which is the exact duplicate in every detail of its former physical body.

[1] *A General Survey of Psychical Phenomena*, Lambert.

Chapter XVIII

AUTOMATIC WRITING

Automatic Writing — "Scripts produced without the control of the conscious self. It is one of the most common forms of mediumship, the source of innumerable cases of self-delusion, and at the same time one of the most valuable of spiritual gifts. If reliable it opens up a direct channel for obtaining teaching from the Beyond."[1]

AUTOMATIC WRITING:

This is a type of psychic phenomena in which the hand of the automatist writes with pencil and paper, without writer's knowing what is to be or has been written, until it has been read after it has been produced. The production of this writing varies all the way from mental suggestion to absolute control of the hand and arm, or even deep unconscious trance. Obviously this method is open to much criticism, as the communication may have originated in the subconscious mind of the automatist, or have been given by telepathy from some other living person. It also affords a great opportunity for the expression of subconscious desires, and a wide field for the manifestation of a lively imagination. Consequently a large percentage of such writings are not communications with the deceased which they purport to represent. Hence all such writings must be judged by their content and the circumstances under which they were produced.

To be properly called automatic writing, the hand of the

---

[1] *The Encyclopoedia of Psychic Science*, Fodor.

automatist must be more or less completely controlled by the discarnate entity with whom he desires to communicate. Such control in its negative aspect may be gradually increased to complete control of the entire body, to the point of complete possession or obsession. On the constructive side the control may become less and less and the consciousness of the automatist, having no knowledge whatever of the message, may respond to the point where the words which follow are anticipated, and where they can be written down or not at the will of the writer.

This can further progress to the point where the message can be clearly understood and written down entirely independent of the control. Naturally this is no longer automatic writing, but becomes voluntary. At this stage it is called inspirational writing as it is now entirely under the control of the automatist and not the discarnate entity. Those who strive to develop this gift should therefore seek to obtain *inspirational* writing instead of the automatic type. In other words the idea the communicator desires to express is impressed upon the mind of the writer by telepathy in his own language instead of that which is characteristic of the communicator, and is then written down or not as the automatist desires. Many noted authors testify that their best writings are obtained this way. Harriet Beecher Stowe, the author of *Uncle Tom's Cabin*, said that she did not write that book for her hand was the instrument of another personality.

LETTERS FROM A LIVING DEAD MAN:

One of the most noted examples of automatic writing is found in the three volumes written by this method by the well known author, Elsa Barker. As she describes their origin, "One night last year, in Paris, I was strongly impelled to take up a pencil and write, although what I was to write about I had no idea. Yielding to the impulse, my hand was seized as if from the outside, and a remarkable message of a personal nature came, followed by the signature, 'X'.... X was not a Spiritualist, I am not myself, and never have been a Spiritualist. . . . Spiritualism had always left me quite cold." But in spite of this indifference Mrs. Barker was impelled to write through this method, three important volumes, *Letters From a Living Dead Man, War Letters From a Living Dead Man,* and *Last Letters From a Living Dead Man.* The controlling influence Mr. X proved to be a Judge Hatch, and much of the information given was entirely unknown to Mrs. Barker, and hence could not have come from her subconscious mind, but must have come from the discarnate intelligence of Judge Hatch.

"He was not an ordinary person. He was a well known lawyer. . . . a profound student of philosophy, a writer of books."

Mrs. Barker says again. "While writing these books I was generally in a state of semi-consciousness, so that until I read the message over afterwards, I had only a vague idea of what it contained. . . . References were often made to past events and the references were afterwards verified. This leaves untouched the favorite telepathic theory of the psychologists. . . . In the absence of X and without some other entity on the invisible side of Nature, in whom I had a like degree of confidence, I could not produce another document of this kind."[2]

How It Is Done:

This is how the discarnate spirit of Judge Hatch speaks of the automatic writing, through the hand of Mrs. Barker:

"By writing with your hand, I am not making any opening through your nervous system through which irresponsible and evil forces can enter and take possession of you. At first I used your hand and arm from the outside, sometimes with such force as to make them lame the next day. . . . Then I tried another method, and you noticed a change in the character of the writing. . . . a third method. . . . I enter your

[2] See *Letters From a Living Dead Man,* Barker.

mind by putting myself in absolute rapport with your mind, impressing upon your mind itself the things I wish to say."[3]

Some of this automatic writing is that of Frederic Myers, the well known leader in psychical research and one of the founders of the Society for Psychical Research, and many of his closest friends, and fearless investigators have believed it to be *his writing*.[4]

Prominent bank officials have identified the handwriting and signatures of Myers and other trusted spirit "writers" whose integrity while on the earth plane was beyond doubt, and who, before their passing had made arrangements by which the officers of the Society would be able to identify them should they find it possible to carry on communications from the spirit world.

EXAMPLES OF AUTOMATIC WRITING:

Among the many cases of notable volumes having been written in truly automatic style, may be mentioned that of *Patience Worth*. This case puzzled not only psychical researchers, but scientists and psychologists also, and those who opposed the after-death-survival theory, were given in this instance a difficult case to explain away. Patience Worth,—purporting to be a peasant girl, who had lived in early life in Dorsetshire, England, and to be killed by Indians in America when she migrated there in the Seventeenth Century—, controlled Mrs. John Curran, a medium of St. Louis, Mo. This woman's education had been limited; her reading never exceeded that of the average American woman of her class and she had travelled little.

She first performed on the ouija-board, but later took to communicating and dictating in direct speech, a number of books of outstanding literary merit, with extreme rapidity, over a wide range of subjects. Among the most notable was *Telka*, a seventy thousand word poem, in the Anglo-Saxon

---

[3] See *Letters From A Living Dead Man*, Barker.
[4] See *The Widow's Mite*, Funk, 484-5.

language of three centuries ago, dictated for the purpose of proving Patience Worth to be a personality independent of the medium, as in it she did not use any words that had come into use since her day. This she considered beyond the powers of anyone now living in this world.

Professor Schiller of Oxford University observed, regarding the antiquated language of *Telka*: "It is certainly impressive to be told that in one of her tales, *Telka*. . . . exhibits a vocabulary up to ninety percent of the Anglo-Saxon origin, and contains no word of later entry into the language of 1600, except the word 'amuck',—which is first recorded in the second half of the seventeenth century—, and no word wrongly formed among those which are on record.

"Professor Allison of the University of Manitoba, who personally studied the case, thought she must be 'the oustanding phenomena of the age," and Dr. Usher, Professor of History in Washington University, considered *The Sorry Tale*, a work of 350,000 words, the greatest story penned of the current life and times since the *Gospels* were published."[5]

William Blake in the preface to his great poem *Jerusalem*, wrote that it was dictated to him. "The grandest poem that this world contains; I may praise it since I dare not pretend to be other than the *secretary*. I have written this poem from immediate dictation, twelve or sometimes twenty or thirty lines at a time, without premeditation and even against my will."[6]

One of the most voluminous examples of automatic writing ever produced was Hudson Tuttle's *Arcana of Nature*, from which Charles Darwin quoted in his *Origin of Species*. Coleridge confessed that his famous poem *Kubla Kahn* was written practically under psychic dictation.

Dickens, Balzac, Victor Hugo, etc., are among the many noted writers who wrote in truly automatic style.

---

[5] See *One Hundred Cases of Survival After Death*, Baird, 99, 100, 101.
[6] *Encyclopedia of Psychic Science*, Fodor.

In the *State of Remembrance* by Bligh Bond, it is related that the automatic writing of his colleague, Captain J. Allen Bartlett, Johannes,—a Glastonbury monk of the 15th century,—revealed to the architects the exact location of the Edgar Chapel of that great Cathedral which had been in ruins for many centuries and the exact location of which there was no record. Subsequent excavations showed that the locations indicated were exact in every detail. Since no persons then living knew of this location, the information could not have been received by telepathy from anyone on earth and therefore must have come from the discarnate monk Johannes, as was claimed.

The late Albert Peyson Terhune is continuing his literary work beyond the grave, his widow says. In her book *Across the Line*, Anice Terhune holds conversation by automatic writing with her husband in the spirit world. She says he speaks to her in a voice closely resembling the one he had while he was alive. While he is interested in his new life, he is not so preoccupied with it that he hasn't taken an interest in her affairs on earth. She had lost some important papers; he told her where to find them.[7]

As another example of automatic writing the following is given from the pen of the Rev. G. Vale Owen a clergyman of impeccable character and deep sincerity of purpose and conviction:

"There is an opinion abroad that the clergy are very credulous beings. . . . but our training. . . . places us among the most hard to convince, when any new truth is in question. It took a quarter of a century to convince me. . . . that spirit communication is a fact, and that the fact was legitimate and good. From the moment I had taken my decision the answer began to appear. First my wife developed the power of automatic writing. Then through her I received requests that I would sit quietly, pencil in hand, and take down

---

[7] See *Washington Post*, Oct. 16th, 1945.

any thoughts which seemed to come into my mind, projected there by some external personality, and not consequent on the exercise of my own mentality."[8]

The script which follows, and from which we have
given excerpts in another chapter, he refers to as being
transmitted by *inspirational writing*, rather than by *automatic writing*.

Ouija Board:

Another method of automatic writing, and one that may
be used outside of the séance room, and by others than
mediums, is the well known but sometimes scoffed-at ouija
board. This little article is too well known and universally used to need description, and is too often used by
the inexperienced seeker after sensation. But some of the
best automatists find this method very effective, and have
received many splendid and worthwhile messages, given
and directed authentically by a spirit visitor.

Mrs. Hestor Travers-Smith, one of the better known
automatic writers, found the ouija board very satisfactory
in her work as a medium and automatic writer. She usually
worked with another automatist and both were blindfolded.
The words came so fast that in most cases, the services of
an experienced stenographer were required to take them
down. This blindfold method has the great advantage of
barring any subconscious guidance of the indicator or
board.

When a pencil thrust through the pointed end of the
ouija board is used to write the message, it is called a
planchette.

In spite of the scoffs at the ouija board it is considered
authentic, and a splendid means of communication with
the other world. It is coming more and more into its own.

"I am inclined to believe that the ouija board may take
honorable place with Sir Isaac Newton's apple. Watt's tea-
kettle, Benjamin Franklin's kite, and many other historic
playthings which have led to many great results.

[8] *The Life Beyond the Vale*, Owen, 8-9.

"This book too started with a ouija board but it does not linger on that phase. . . . Betty blindfolded her eyes, or looked away from the paper, so that she might seperate herself as far as possible from what was to come next."[9]

---
[9] *The Betty Book*, White, 15-22.

CHAPTER XIX

TELEGRAPHIC MESSAGES AND OTHER PHYSICAL PROOFS

As we have stated before, it has been proven by scientific investigation that while the Astral World is a locality in space in relation to the Physical World, it is also a state of matter of a higher vibration than that in which the Physical World manifests. As we have mentioned in a previous chapter, materialized astral bodies from the Spirit World have been repeatedly weighed and photographed, in scientific laboratories, under the strictest test conditions, which settles the question as to the *reality* and *material nature* of the substance of that world.

The following cases of phenomena, produced in the séance room and elsewhere, are strong proofs of this statement of the actual substance of the spirit body:[1]

TELEGRAPHIC MESSAGES:

Telegraphic messages are messages received from the other world through mediumship, on telegraphic machines and on typewriters. We use these phenomena as further proof of personal survival and of the *real substance and reality* of the discarnate entity which comes down from the spirit world to give us proof of his personal survival after death.

An electrical instrument has been devised by David Wilson, M.A. of Cambridge, England, on the order of a telegraph

---

[1] For further details *Realms of the Living Dead*, Curtiss, 24-5.

PLATE XXIX—Precipitated painting of "Ida."

instrument over which he has received hundreds of independent communications in all languages. In this experiment the familiar Morse Code was used, typed out by the materialized hands of those who have returned to this plane from the Spirit World. This adds much to the weight of testimony to prove that those who have left the Physical World through "death" may and do have communication with those of us here who are willing to open our minds to the possibility of such communication, and that the Spirit body does have material substance and actual strength enough to manipulate a telegraphic instrument or other mechanical contrivance.[1]

MANIPULATION OF THE TYPEWRITER:

One of the most remarkable cases of manipulation of a physical instrument by the hands of an unseen *guest* from the Spirit World was received through the mediumship of Miss Lizzie Bangs, one of the famous mediums *"The Bangs Sisters"* of Chicago. A typewriter in the séance room was held in the air by four men, and was operated by *materialized hands from the other side*. These hands could be plainly seen by the men holding the machine.

PAINTINGS FROM THE SPIRIT WORLD:

It was also under the mediumship of the Bangs sisters that the famous painting of the spirit guide "Ida," guide of Vice-Admiral W. Osborne Moore, was *painted* by the unseen hands of a discarnate spirit. We produce herein a picture of the painting, which was obtained under strict test conditions and in the presence of Admiral Moore.[2]

OTHER PROOFS:

This use of the hands in painting together with *loud* rappings, the tilting and lifting of objects too heavy to be lifted

---

[1] *Occult Review*, June 1917.
[2] *Psychic Observer*, Jan. 25th, 1945.

by human hands, the use of the electrical instrument, the manipulation of the hands of the writer in automatic writing, the control of the action of the ouija board, etc., all give strong evidence of the reality of the strength and substance of the discarnate visitor from the spirit-plane.

CHAPTER XX

POLYGLOT LANGUAGES, CROSS CORRESPONDENCE AND BOOK TESTS

In addition to the phenomenon of the direct voice itself, the fact that it speaks in many different languages through the medium who knows only one language is of itself another physical proof of personal survival. This form of psychic phenomenon is known as Polyglot Language or Zenoglossis.

EXAMPLES:

In a recent article we are told, "There are literally hundreds of such evidential type cases of direct contact between persons who speak one or more foreign languages with their relatives or friends from the spiritual planes, persons who speak through their medium as plainly as if they were on our side of life.

"Here is one Mr. Skeptic will have to twist and turn through a mental labyrinth to explain,—in his terms. A Scottish-born lady, who had attended the Rev. Zenor's meetings only a few times, was surprised one evening when a voice spoke to her in Gaelic, the traditional language of the Scots. She immediately recognized the Gaelic phrase for '*How are you*' and she replied in kind. Then the voice spoke her name in Gaelic and she knew the proper reply—the name of the street where she formerly lived. The voice completed the address with the name of the town, the Gaelic form for *Inverness, Scotland*.

"Observations of the speakers of foreign languages through

the trance mediumship of the Rev. Zenor have been greatly augmented by the experiences of another researcher, an M.D. who fortunately speaks no less than eight languages and has a working knowledge of several others.

Languages Spoken:

"He has carried on conversations with persons speaking through the mediums in such languages as *French*, *German*, *Russian*, *Norwegian*, *Spanish*, *Chinese* (*Cantonese*), and Polish, which he speaks fluently. He has also been able to distinguish the words of the speakers of *Japanese*, the *Manchu* and *Mandarin* forms of *Chinese*, *Tibetan* and *Swedish* all of which he understands well enough to know that they are being properly spoken. He has even carried on conversations in *Lithuanian*! Furthermore, at least one speaker has voiced phrases which are identifiable as an *ancient form of Chinese*.

"In addition a member of his family speaks *Bohemian* or *Czech*, as well as *Polish*, and has carried on extensive conversations in these languages with persons speaking through the Rev. Zenor."[1]

Constant repetition of the phenomenon has been strikingly demonstrated, for thousands of such messages in foreign languages are obtained through mediums every year, and recognized by their grateful recipients as completely evidential.

An English medium, Mr. Lowenthal, testified that he was frequently made to speak in the language of another nation which he believed to be the tongue of the North American Indian. He says: "My mouth utters sounds that I do not understand, and which have no meaning to me.[2]

Mrs. Young, a medium of Chicago, under the control of German spirits, sang and spoke *German* in a circle in which no one knew that language. At other times she spoke in *Span-*

---

[1] *Psychic Observer*, Oct. 25th, 1944.
[2] *Encyclopedia of Psychic Science*, Fodor, 411.

ish and *Italian*, although she was an uneducated woman who knew neither of these languages.[3]

Miss Laura Edmonds, the daughter of the famous medium and psychical investigator, Judge John Worth Edmonds of New York, developed this "gift of tongues" after she became a medium. Although she knew and spoke only *English*, and a small amount of *French*, she spoke fluently many different languages while in trance. Some of these were identified as *Spanish, French, Greek, Italian, Portugese* and *Hungarian*, and others entirely foreign to her native English tongue.[4]

Miss Jenny Keyes, another well known medium, while in trance *sang* in *Spanish* and *Italian*. Others frequently sang and spoke in *Hebrew*, *Greek*, *Malay*, *Chinese* and *Indian*, although none of them could converse in these languages while out of trance.

The New York Evening Post of Nov. 10th, 1930, reported the case of a little four-year-girl at Warsaw who, though her parents spoke only Polish, developed the extraordinary habit of talking to herself in a foreign tongue which no one about her could understand but which was later detected to be pure *Gaelic*. It is interesting that her great-grandfather came from the land of the Hebrides and spoke Gaelic before he came to Warsaw.

Frequently the mediums will *write* a message in a foreign language of which they have no knowledge or understanding while out of the trance state. The young daughter of Mr. and Mrs. Brown of Melbourne, eleven years old, wrote some Chinese characters holding the pen in Chinese fashion.

There are many other such cases of writing by discarnate spirits, in another language than that known by the medium, in the annals of Psychical research, which go to prove again the actuality of personal survival.

---

[3] *Thirty Years of Psychical Research*, Richet, 222.
[4] *Encyclopedia of Psychical Research*, Fodor, 118.

OTHER EVIDENCES:

In addition to those given there are other types of evidence which, while not to be counted as *physical proofs*, are nevertheless additional evidence. One of these is furnished when only part of a message is given through one medium, which is of itself incomplete, and another sentence is given through another medium to complete the message.

Still another evidence is given by having certain words on certain pages in a specified book pointed out, which will convey testimony of the presence of the communicator.[5]

CROSS CORRESPONDENCE:

Cross correspondence is that found in the script of two or more automatic writers acting without collusion and under such conditions that the possibility of communication by normal means is removed. They are messages given to one medium in part, and the rest of the message given to another without collaboration as to the message on the part of the mediums.

The theory—to eliminate from mediumistic communication the hypothesis of telepathy between the living—has been credited to the celebrated deceased scholar, F. W. H. Myers, after his death in 1901.

On one occasion a long message was sent to him in Latin. He gave fragments of his reply through three different mediums at various times none of which alone made sense, but which when pieced together gave the correct reply.

Miss Johnson of the Society of Psychical Research who made a very close study of Cross Correspondence, on studying the script of five or more mediums concerning the same message, thus describes the conclusion she came to:

"The characteristics of these cases. . . . —or at least some of them,—is that we do not get in the writing of one automatist anything like a mechanical verbatim reproduction of the phrases in the other. We do not even get the same idea ex-

---

[5] *Encyclopedia of Psychical Knowledge*, Fodor.

pressed in different ways as well might result from direct telepathy between them. What we do get is a fragmentary utterance in one script, which seems to have no particular point or meaning, and another fragmentary utterance in the other, of an equally pointless character; but when we put the two together, we see that they supplement one another, and that there is apparently one coherent idea underlying both, but only partially expressed in each."[6]

BOOK TESTS:

Book-tests is a curious phenomenon destined to eliminate telepathy from the living as an alternative explanation to the survival theory. It is in a certain sense an offshoot or extension of the cross-correspondence idea.

The newspaper tests of Mr. C Brayton Thomas, which he conducted with the celebrated trance medium Mrs. Osborne Leonard, are similar in idea to book-tests. The communicating intelligences gave names one day which were printed in certain columns and pages of the next day's *Times*, and the results obtained were very striking, as neither the composer nor the editor of that paper could tell *at the hour of Mr. Thomas' sitting*, just what particular item would appear in the next day's issue.[7]

Another experiment on book-tests is given as follows. Lord Glenconner of England, had given special study to forestry, and was especially interested in the damaging effect a type of tunnelling beetle has on young trees. His son "Bim," who had been killed in the battle of the Somme in 1916, was well aware of this fact. Through the mediumship of Mrs. Osborne Leonard, he sent a message to his father, telling him to look for the "ninth book on the third shelf, counting from left to right in a certain bookcase, on the right of the door of the drawing room." The book indicated proved to be *Trees*. He was told to "rake" the title and look at page "37." On the

---

[6] *History of Spiritualism*, Doyle, 78.
[7] *A General Survey of Psychic Phenomena*, Lambert, 27.

bottom of page 36 and the top of 37, were the words: "Sometimes you will see curious marks in the wood; these are caused by a tunnelling beetle, very injurious to the trees. . . . ."

This test proved so satisfactory to Bim's family that he was a communicator and that he was present with them, that it brought a glow of happy satisfaction to all present.[8]

---

[8] *Encyclopedia of Psychical Knowledge*, Fodor.

Chapter XXI

HOUDINI'S TEST MESSAGE

Many people interested in exposing fraud, and also in giving credit to those sincere workers who seek to establish the truth about life after death put their experiments to every test in order not only to expose the fraudulent but to verify the authenticity of those who really do communicate with spirit friends come back from the Spirit World, to tell us of the life over there and to comfort and sustain the loved ones left behind, and also to prove that they are not only still alive but retain their own individuality.

One of the better ways to do this is to arrange and formulate, while those interested are still on the Earth Plane, some sort of secret code or signal known only to the interested parties and to be used between them when one or the other goes over to the Spirit World.

By this means they are able to prove not only that those on the other side can and do return to communicate with those left on the Earth Plane, but also to *establish the identity* of the spirit visitor.

HOUDINI'S MESSAGE:

One of the most remarkable examples of this kind of test is shown in the test messages of the late Harry Houdini.

This well known magician Harry Weiss, better known by his stage name of "Harry Houdini," did a great service to Spiritualism by exposing many fraudulent mediums. On the other hand he took every occasion he could in his public performances to discredit Spiritualism by his claim that *all* mediums were frauds, and that any communication with the deceased was impossible. In an effort to prove this he arranged with his wife a secret code message which he was to deliver after his death if such a thing were at all possible. After his death, messages were received through several mediums which purported to be the test message. All of these were denied by the wife. Sometime later, however, fragmentary messages were received from him through the Rev. Arthur Ford, a word at a time. First, however, a key word to the whole sequence – FORGIVE – was brought through from his mother. This word Mrs. Houdini acknowledged over her signature to be the key word, and to be the only correct word received among thousands of messages purporting to be from him.

Had this word been received from his mother by Houdini during his lifetime, it might have altered the whole course of his investigation, for it would have proved to him that communication with the "dead" was possible, and so might have prevented his attempt to discredit all such messages.

The first word of the second message was given to a group of friends sitting with Arthur Ford early in November 1928. The message in its entirety came through during eight separate sittings, covering a period of two and one half months.

The method employed by Fletcher, the medium's control, was to give out the words as they came and as the opportunity offered. Seldom more than one word came at a time at the beginning, and frequently the intervals were as far as two weeks apart.

"The first word 'ROSABELLE' " said Fletcher, "is the one that is going to unlock the rest." Two weeks later a second word was added, "NOW," and on December 18th, another word. . . . this word was "LOOK.". . . . "

In the group-sitting next to the final one of January 5th, when the message was delivered complete, and in the correct sequence, Fletcher said. "Let me give you the words from the beginning, because I have to work hard to get them."

The details of the development, or gradual building up of this message taken mostly from stenographic records of the sittings are given in order that those most interested may know that the message did not arrive full grown.

At the final sitting on the evening of January 5th. . . . Fletcher continued, "It has been a hard job getting them through, but I tell you," he said, "they are right!! ". . . . Fletcher continued, "A man who says he is Houdini but whose real name was Ehrich Weiss, is here and wishes to send to his wife, Beatrice Houdini, the ten-word code, which he agreed to do if it were possible for him to communicate. He says you are to take this message to her and upon her acceptance of it, he wishes her to follow out the plan they agreed upon before his passing. . . . Then," said Fletcher, "there is something that he wants to tell me that no one but his wife knows. He smiles now and shows me a picture and draws the curtain so! . . . . or in this manner."

That evidently was the clue for the unfoldment of the next part of the code, for Mrs. Houdini responded in French. . . . "and now the nine words besides ROSABELLE spell a word in our code.". . . . Continuing in this way to the end he said: "The message I want to send back to my wife is 'ROSABELLE, BELIEVE!' " "Is that right?" asked Fletcher. "Yes," answered Mrs. Houdini with great feeling.

Fletcher, concluding, repeated that which was being given him: "He says 'tell the whole world that Harry Houdini still lives, and will prove it a thousand times and more.' He is pretty excited. He says, 'I was perfectly honest and sincere, though I resorted to tricks, for the simple reason that I did not believe it true, and no more — tricks — than was justifiable. I am now sincere in sending this through my desire to undo. Tell all those who lost faith because of my mistake, to lay hold again of hope, and to live with the knowledge that life is continuous. That is my message to the world through my wife and through this instrument.' "

The day after the receipt of this message, Mrs. Houdini issued the following statement at her home!

"Regardless of all statements to the contrary, I wish to declare that the message, in its entirety, and in the agreed upon sequence, given to me by Arthur Ford, is the correct message pre-arranged between Mr. Houdini and myself.

(signed)

Beatrice Houdini"

Witnessed
   Harry R. Zander,
   Minnie Chester,
   John W. Stafford.

. . . . Fletcher went on to say "This last is the message which was to go to his wife. He wants it signed in ink by each one present. He says the code is known only to him and his wife, and that no one on earth knew it but these two. He says there is no danger on that score and that she must make it public. 'It must come from her; you are nothing more than agents.' He says that when this comes through there will be a veritable storm, that many will seek to destroy her, and that she will be accused of everything that is not good, but she is honest enough to keep the pact which they repeated over and over before his death. The last words he spoke were those used in going over this together so that they would both understand it clearly. 'I know,' he says, 'That she will be happy because neither of us believed it would be possible.' "

Two members of the group, Mr. Fast and Mr. Stafford, both strangers to Mrs. Houdini, as were all of the sitters, delivered the message to her at her home the following day. . . . Dropping the letter to her side and stirred with emotion, she said, "It is right!" Asking for more details concerning the message, she then undertook to carry out the plan agreed upon with her husband. The medium Arthur Ford, accompanied by three members of his group, and a representative of the United Press, went to Mrs. Houdini's home and with two of her friends gathered at her side.

In a short time the voice of Fletcher came through. "This man is coming now," he says, "the same one who came the other night. He tells me to say, 'Hello Bess, Sweetheart,' and he wants to repeat the message and finish it for you. 'The code,' he says, 'is one you used to use in one of your secret mindreading acts.' Repeating the ten words to her, he said, "He wants you to tell him whether they are right or not! "Yes," replied Mrs. Houdini, "they are." He smiles and says, 'Thank you.' "Now I can go on," continued Fletcher. "He tells you to take off your wedding ring and tell them what Rosabelle means." Drawing her left hand from under the cover she took off the ring, and holding it before her she sang in a small voice, 'Rosabelle' etc. . . ."

Mrs. Houdini's attitude has been that of an honest skeptic who had no alternative but to accept the message once it was the one agreed upon. She has stoutly maintained in the face of the crudest opposition, that no one but herself could probably have known the contents of the message sealed in her vault. Even close friends urged that at any cost she deny the message as the correct one on the plea that it would undo all that her husband had stood for. To this she replied, "It was what he wanted me to do and I am doing it. Nothing will change my belief until it is proved some other way." She has confirmed conclusively that no one but her husband and herself could possibly have known the details of the code; that neither openly nor covertly could it have been gleaned.

Some years later pressure was brought to bear on Mrs. Houdini to repudiate her former statements as to the correct transmission of the message agreed upon with her husband. But no amount of later denial can alter the fact of or disallow her signed statement and the unanimous testimony of those present at the séance.

Note—All of the above quotations and data are taken from *The Houdini Messages*, Fast.

CHAPTER XXII

OTHER PHYSICAL PHENOMENA

There are other physical phenomena which we will talk about in this chapter which add their testimony and assurance to the great accumulation of proof of personal survival of what we call death.

APPORTS:

Apports is the term applied to objects which through psychic power are phenomenally brought into the presence of a materializing medium, thereby establishing the fact of the passage of matter through matter, since the doors and windows of the séance room are usually locked and sealed.

These apports embrace a wide variety of articles, the most common of which are flowers, semi-precious stones—cut and uncut—and coins, ancient and modern. Other objects are clay tablets bearing cuneiform inscriptions from excavations at ancient Babylon, Indian blankets, tomahawks, human scalp locks and even human beings.

Charles Bailey who specialized in materializing living objects apported such things as crabs, turtles, a thirty-inch live snake, a ten-inch baby shark and a nest full of birds with the mother bird still on it. The nest and mother bird were later apported back whence they came, live birds are often felt flying about in the darkened room, the most common ones being doves and jungle sparrows. Tropical birds are often brought in cages.

PLATE XXX—Ivy plant apported July 15th, 1928 at Millesimo Castle.

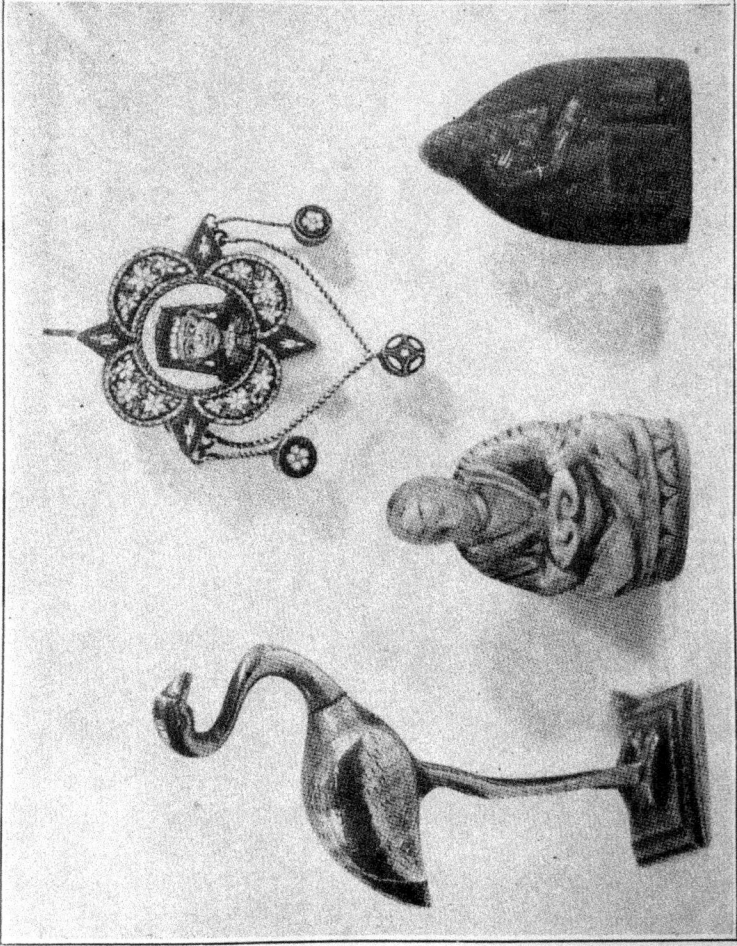

PLATE XXXI—These articles, a brass bird, a stone Buddha, a Mosaic ornament, and an Egyptian ornament of Osiris, were apported at the séances of Jack Weber.

Probably the most common apport is flowers, often in the midst of winter. A famous medium, Mrs. Guppy, once materialized boughs of orange blossoms and an armful of flowers with more than forty live butterflies on them. She also materialized a block of ice a foot square, and many other objects too numerous to mention. Alfred Russell Wallace once requested her to obtain a sunflower for him. In less than five minutes a sunflower seven feet tall, and with a large amount of earth clinging to its roots, was deposited on the table.

At a séance of "Margery" in Boston, her brother Walter was asked to obtain a living flower. In a few minutes a golden lily six feet tall, and containing seven large blossoms, was placed on the table. The scent of the flowers was almost overhelming. Upon turning on the lights, the stem of the lily was found to pass through a hole in a large piece of mummy cloth, which was still redolent of the odor of spices. Seven days later, when the lily mysteriously disappeared, the piece of mummy cloth was left behind still with the hole through which the stem passed, but with no tear or slit in it through which the stem might have slipped out.

The Bangs sisters were mediums in whose séances apports of flowers were received, objects disappeared and chemical changes were effected, such as turning ink into dirty water, etc.

ASPORTS:

When the materialized objects called *Apports* are phenomenally removed from the presence of the medium, they are called *Asports*.

Asports often form part of a demonstration of apport phenomena. In one of the Millesimo séances with the Marquis Centurione Scotto and Mme. Fabian Rossi, the members of the circle were tapped by a little parchment drum, and Mme. Rossi and another sitter felt their hands squeezed by two iron mittens. At the conclusion of the séance, these articles were no longer found in the room, but were found in the respective places from which they had been apported.[1]

TRANSPORTS:

When materialized objects, often human beings, are carried from one place to another through closed doors and over a distance, the phenomena are called *Transports*. There are too many thoroughly investigated and authenticated cases of the transportation of human beings to more than mention here so we will cite briefly only the most outstanding cases.

One of the most astonishing of such cases is that of the celebrated Italian materializing medium Marquis Centurione Scotto of Millesimo Castle, whom we have mentioned above. During the course of a sitting, the Marquis was heard to exclaim in a frightened voice: "I can no longer feel my legs!" Some one spoke to him and receiving no answer, the red light was turned on and he was found to be missing from his chair in the séance room, although the door was locked and sealed and the key was in the lock on the inside. After several hours of frantic search, a spirit message through automatic writing said that he could be found in a haymow in the granary in the stable-yard, nearly one hundred yards away from the séance room. There he was found in a deep sleep and was as much astonished and alarmed as any one on realizing his strange position. To reach this position normally, he would have had to pass through three doors which were all found to be locked from the outside.[2]

Another case is that of Mr. Frank Herne, who was transported from his seat in a London theatre, and dropped into a séance room at Hackney, London, several miles distant from the theatre. Later his overcoat, hat, and umbrella, were dropped on the table in the same room.

The record of Mrs. Guppy, "One of the biggest women in London," is probably the best corroborated. At the request of

---

[1] *Modern Psychic Mysteries*, Hack.
[2] *Encyclopedia of Psychic Science*, Fodor.

one of the sitters in a private séance, Katie King, one of
the spirit guides, said she wotdd bring her into the séance
room. Within four minutes there was Mrs. Guppy in their
midst, and much embarrassed at appearing in company
in a loose morning gown and bedroom slippers. She had
been at her desk making up her household accounts and
was brought to the séance with the pen still in her hand and
the ink wet on it. The séance room was more than three
miles from her home, and yet she was transported within
four minutes.[3]

Another remarkable instance was the case of William
Eglinton, who was transported up through the ceiling, and
was found on the floor in the room above.

In still another case, the three children of Senor
Buenaventura Corales frequently vanished from the séance room, found themselves in the garden and were
returned, to their great delight, in the same mysterious
manner. Although the doors were locked in each case, upon
search for them, they were always found outside the séance
room, usually talking and laughing over their adventure.

In the case of two Italian boys, Alfred and Paul Passini,
they experienced mysterious transportation in half an hour,
from Ruvo to Molfetta, and again from Ruvo to a boat at
sea.

In another instance, Dr. Joseph Lapponi tells of the flying brothers of Nari, who could transfer themselves over
a distance of 45 kilometres in fifteen minutes.[4]

According to the Bible these levitations are no new phenomena. In Ezekiel 11, 1: "Moreover the Spirit lifted me
up, and brought me into the East Gate of the Lord's House,
which looked Eastward." Habakkuk was carried from Judea
to Babylon to bring food to Daniel in the Lion's den, and
then carried back to Judea through the air. In the Acts of
the Apostles, the warders of St. Peter's prison, testify: "The
prison house we found shut in all safety, and the keepers

---

[3] *Ibid.*
[4] *Ibid.*

standing before the doors; but when we opened, we found no man within." St. Philip baptized the Ethiopian; "and when they were come up out of the water, the spirit of the Lord caught away Philip, that the eunuch saw him no more. . . . But Philip was found at Axotus." This was a distance of some thirty miles from Gaza the scene of the baptism. As we have pointed out elsewhere, the aged Simeon was apported into the temple in Jerusalem, so he could meet Jesus before he died, as was promised by the Lord. St. Luke, 11: 26-7.

How It Is Done:

As to how apportation, asportation and transportation are accomplished, it must be assumed that there is a hitherto unknown, or fourth aspect of matter, an atomic or fluid condition, in which there is a greater malleability of matter than has been formerly known.

Both through experiment and through the report of spirit guides, it has been found that through psychic forces, the physical object is dematerialized, transported to the desired spot, and then rematerialized. This conclusion is born out by the fact that the thermo-dynamic force required to dematerialize the object is released when it is rematerialized. In the case of metallic objects and stones, this process often makes the object too hot to be handled until it is cooled off. In the case of living beings there must be some other factor involved, as they do not experience this phenomenon of superheating, and yet they have been dematerialized. This is testified by the alarm felt by the Marquis Scotto when he felt for his legs and found them dematerialized, just before he went into a deep trance.

Another case, and a most remarkable one of transport, is told in *One Hundred Cases of Survival After Death*, Baird, page 209. We quote:

"Dr. Paul Gibier, an eminent psychologist and Director of the Pasteur Institute of New York, had a very decisive experience with Mrs. Salmon.

"He experimented in his own laboratory, using an iron cage especially made to his instructions, with a door closing by a lock. Mrs. Salmon was placed in the cage, the door locked, the key put in his pocket, and a stamped paper gummed over the lock. A very short time after the lights were extinguished, hands, arms and living forms came out of the cage, – a man, a woman, more often a lively little girl. Suddenly Mrs. Salmon emerged from the cage and fell half fainting on the floor. The seals were found intact and the door had not been opened."

A remarkable case was the dematerialization and transportation of Charles Victor Miller, at a séance in San Francisco, in the presence of twenty-seven persons. Mr. Miller was apported through the enclosed walls of a séance room and found later,. . . . still in trance, on the second floor. This was done under strictly test conditions.[5]

LEVITATION:

This phenomenon is the familiar one of the lifting of human beings or of objects into the air, contrary to the laws of gravitation, and without any visible agency. *Levitation* is *transportation* in its highest form, and many instances of it are recorded in the Bible, in both the old and new Testament. The record of Jesus' walking on the water, Matthew 14, 24-7 is a splendid illustration, and that many of the saints and other highly intelligent beings accomplished the same feat is a recorded fact.

Levitation is not confined to the séance room, but has been demonstrated in broad daylight, and many authentic cases have been reported of the lifting of tables, chairs and human beings in halls and homes. These latter are very numerous and we cite a few of the best authenticated ones.

Before a very large assembly in a lighted hall, the medium Henry C. Hall was lifted into the air and floated over the

---

[5] *An Occultist Travels*, Reichel.

seats for several minutes and then sank back slowly to the floor.

Three witnesses, the Earl of Dunraven, Lord Lindsay, and Captain Wynne reported that they saw the medium D. D. Home float out through the third story window of one room, and float in through a window of another room. Upon investigation, no ledge or other support on which the body could have rested, could be found. The spectators all agreed that the light in the room was sufficient for them to have detected any outside aid which might have been given. All three were ready to swear to the fact of his having gone out of the window of one room, and having floated in through the window of another room without any visible aid.

Home experienced many other instances of levitation, and was not always in a trance when they occurred. He wrote of his experiences that "he could feel no hands supporting him at any time, and that he felt no sense of fear, even when he was levitated to a great height."[6]

There are so many instances of levitation of objects small and large that there is no necessity of mentioning any of them here. Tables and chairs, and even pianos are moved and levitated into the air at séances and before the astonished eyes of even the most skeptical in ordinary rooms in broad daylight and under the strictest test conditions. In most cases even the most rigid investigations have failed to show that the levitation of these objects could be accomplished by any other means than through the work of discarnate spirits.

POLTERGEISTS:

The phenomenon of *Poltergeists* is a combination of Levitation and Apportation. This term is applied to the physical phenomenon which includes loud raps, poundings, rattling noises, and pranks such as any mischievous child might indulge in. It is applied especially when physical objects are hurled through the air in broad daylight, often with seem-

---

[6] *Encyclopedia of Psychic Science*, Fodor.

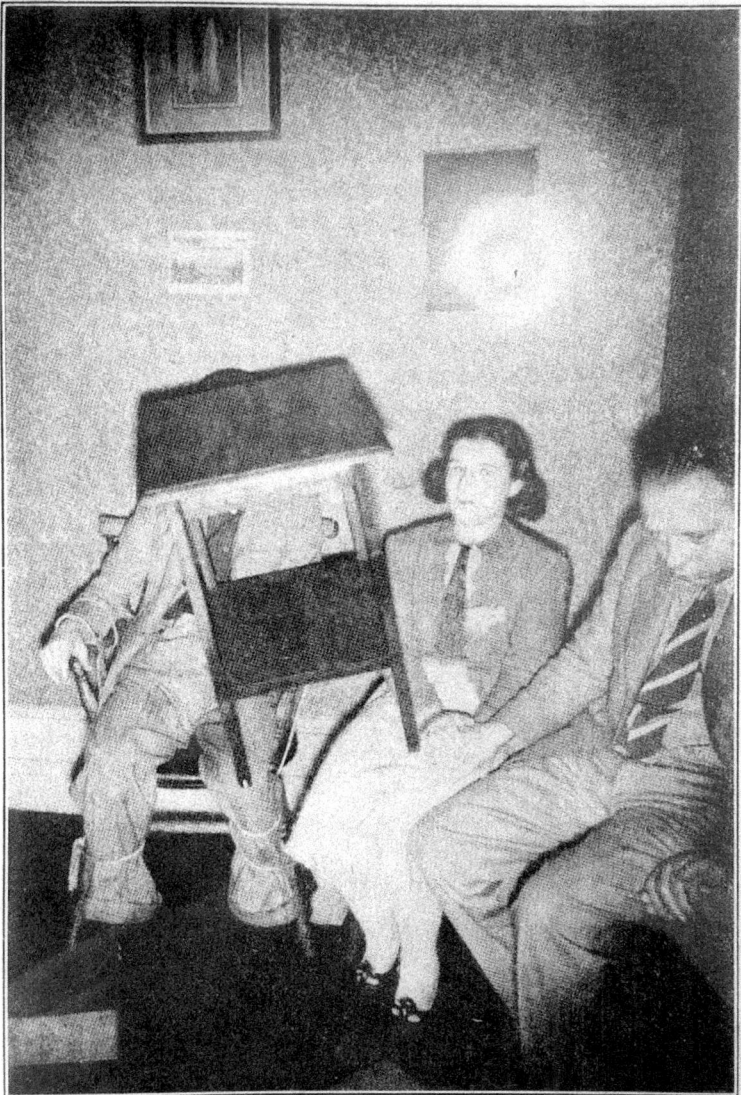

PLATE XXXII—Levitation of a table at the Jack Weber séance in
the presence of Mr. Bernard Gray, a newspaper investigator.

ingly vicious intent. In very extreme cases of this phenomenon, investigating police have been driven from the room
by the force of such flying objects.

Those who manifest Poltergeits seem also to take delight
in such futilities as the breaking of crockery, the throwing
about of furniture, and the materializing of carrots or coal
in the drawing-room. Some cases of this phenomenon are
herein given.

THE EPWORTH PHENOMENA:

These disturbances occurred at the vicarage of the
Rev. Samuel Wesley, father of John Wesley, the founder
of Methodism, and were attested to by the whole Wesley
family all of whom were decidedly psychic. These phenomena, lasting over a period of more than two months,
include loud knocks and poundings, the sound of a board
being planed as if by a carpenter, the sound of crashing
china in the kitchen, where no china was found broken,
and the sound of many people tramping up and down the
stairs with heavy shoes. The two men attributed these per-
secutions to the devil, but Mrs. Wesley and her daughter
claimed they were due to her brother "Old Jeffery," who
had passed away in India some years previous to the disturbances. It is said that for some time visitors were shown
large blotches of ink on the wall of John Wesley's study
where he had thrown an ink bottle at a "persecuting devil."[1]

The case of the Joller family in Stans, Switzerland,
gives us a most convincing and formidable array of evidence of this phenomenon. In the home of M. Joller, a
prominent lawyer and a man of splendid character, a
series of disturbances broke out, such as loud knocks,
sounds of sobbing, and the opening of windows and
doors by invisible hands. Cupboard drawers were
pulled out and left in disorderly fashion, and the family were annoyed by strange gray shapes roaming about
the house. These manifestations continued over a long

---

[1] *Encyclopedia of Psychic Science*, Fodor.

period, and were witnessed by many persons other than the family, persons who hearing of the strange phenomena were attracted to the house. Many of these were prominent people such as the Director of Police and the President of the Court of Justice, Stans. The strange happenings went on outside the house as well as inside, and in broad daylight, which precluded the possibility of fraud. There seemed no way of overcoming these strange and uncomfortable happenings until M. Joller and his family were forced to vacate the home and find other living quarters.[2]

Poltergeists usually take place where there is a sensitive child in the family, especially when there is a young girl who is just entering puberty, but it is not definitely known whether this condition is a causative factor or is merely a coincidence. The phenomena are largely attributed to disembodied, mischievous children who delight to tease, or to low grade morons who desire thus to plague their superiors and take these methods of attracting attention to themselves.[3]

---

[2] *Encyclopedia of Occultism*, Spence.
[3] *Ibid.*

Chapter XXIII

LETTERS FROM HELL

NOTE TO THE READER: If you have recently lost a dear one by Graduation from earth-life, do not connect the experiences related in this chapter with your loved one, for they will probably have no relation to the conditions through which your own is passing.

We also recommend the reader not to read this chapter at night, unless it is immediately followed by the reading of the next chapter. *Letters From Heaven*, before laying the book down, or else by repeating the *Prayer For Protection*,[1] or by reading some chapter in the Bible such as the 23rd Psalm.

The text of the book *Letters From Hell*, of which portions of this chapter is a condensation, was written by a Spanish medium in 1882, and passed through several editions in various other languages. It is condensed and placed here because of the power of its truth to give concrete understanding of the conditions that are described in the Bible, as eternal torment, generally spoken of as *Hell*. This description is necessary to complete our account of all after-death conditions, even the lowest, in which the dregs of humanity exist until through suffering they have progressed out of them.

In the preface the English translator says: "When I say that the book is full of truth, I do not mean other truth of theory or truth in art but something far deeper and higher — the realities of our relations to God and man and duty — all,

---

[1] *See Prayers*, Curtiss.

in short, that belongs to the *conscience*. Prominent among these is the awful verity, that *we make our fate in unmaking ourselves; that men, in defacing the image of God in themselves, construct for themselves a world of horror and dismay; that our own deeds and character are the informing or inwardly creating cause of the outer Darkness; that if a man will not have God he can never be rid of his weary and hateful self."*

The book has a fearful title and is far more fearful than its title; but if it will help to turn any away from that which alone is *really horrible*, the doing of unrighteousness, it will prove itself the outcome of a Divine energy of deliverance. We quote:

I had lived a life of selfishness, ever pleasing my own desire. It was true, awfully true, that I had not followed the way of life, but the path of death, since the days even of childhood. And now I lay dying, a victim of my own folly, wretched, hopelessly lost! One after another my sins rose before me, crying for expiation; but it was too late now—too late for repentance. Despair only was left; the very thought of repentance had faded from the brain.

An unknown sensation laid hold of me. What was this I felt? Death had clutched my every fibre, but I seemed released, free, strangely free! Consciousness had been fading but was returning even now, waking as from a swoon.

But consciousness at first seemed returned chiefly to experience an indescribable feeling of nakedness, which indeed might explain the terrible cold assailing me. . . . I still believed in my personal identity but I was merely a shadow of myself. The eye which saw, the teeth which chattered, did not exist any more than the rest of my earthly body existed. All that was left of me was an astral shade, unclothed to the skin,—nay to the inmost soul. . . . No wonder I shivered; no wonder I felt naked. But the feeling of nakedness, strong as it was, excluded shame. . . . I had died and found myself in hell!. . . . in that place of weeping and gnashing of teeth, of torment, alas! beyond conception. This then, was the end of life's enjoyment.

In spite of the self-love which had accompanied me hither, unimpaired, I hated myself with a burning implacable hatred. . . . I felt sad, I felt ruined and miserably undone. I condemned, I cursed. But repentance was far from me. . . . The power of repentance was lost! And remembering the many so-called good intentions of my sinful soul, I felt ready to tear myself to pieces. In sooth, I myself had assisted diligently in paving the road to hell! But that feeling was devoid of contrition. . . .

I started suddenly; there was a young woman beside me with a babe on her arm.

"It is hopeless trying," she said almost tenderly. "I myself have tried it, and tried again; but it's no use. There is no water here, not as much as a single tear." Alas I felt she spoke the truth. . . . I longed to weep but could not. . . . The young woman sat down beside me. Indescribably touching was the expression of sorrowing fondness with which she gazed upon the babe in her lap, a tiny thing which apparently had not lived many days. . . .

"Don't you think my baby is still alive," she said. "It is not dead, it is asleep!"

To tell the truth I thought the baby was dead but I had it not in me to grieve the poor creature, so I said, "It may be asleep—babies do sleep a great deal."

"Yes, yes, it is asleep," she repeated softly, rocking the child. "They say I killed my child, my own little baby," she continued. "But don't you think they talk foolishly? How could a mother find it in her heart to kill her child, her very own child?" and she pressed the little thing to her bosom, with convulsive tenderness. The sight was more than I could endure and I rose and left her. Yet it soothed my own misery that for a moment I seemed filled with another's grief, rather than my own. Her grief I could leave behind. I fled, but my own wretchedness followed on my heels. . . .

I seemed to be in front of a tavern. . . . they were making merry within. . . . drinking, gambling, making merry and what-not. . . .

But it was an awful merriment in which those horrible astral shades were engaged. . . . The landlord beckoned me to enter; an inviting fire was blazing on the hearth, and shivering as I was I went towards it. . . . "Can't you come in by the door?" he snarled. . . .

I stammered, "I am so cold, so miserably cold!"

"The more fool you for going naked," cried the fellow, with an ugly grin. "We admit only well dressed people as a rule." Involuntarily I thought of my warm clothing, and scarcely had the idea been shaped in my brain, I found myself clothed. . . . At the same time my nakedness was not covered and I felt as cold as before. I moved towards the hearth, and put my trembling hands to the grate. . . . The blaze emitted no warmth. . . . I turned away in despair. The merry-making shades laughed harshly, calling me a fool for my pains. One of them handed me a goblet. . . . I seized the cup and lifted it to my lips, that I might drain it. Alas! the nothingness! My burning desire found it an empty cup, and I felt ready to faint.

"What house is this?. . . . It's my house. How did it come to be here?". . . . The landlord looked at me with a sneer. . . . "How did it come to be here? — Why I thought of it and there it was. Then the house is merely an idea? Yes, of course. Here we are in the true land of magic. We need but imagine a thing and then we have it. . . . ."

One thing only was no empty idea, but fearful reality — the terrible necessity which forced these shadowy semblances of men to appear to be doing now, in the spirit, the very things they did in the body upon earth. . . .

It is impossible for me to tell you to what extent a man here may shrink together within himself. . . . I cowered as a toad in a hole, hugging my miserable being, until I was aroused by a groan coming from somewhere beside me. I

started affrighted and looked about; the darkness being still
increasing, I. . . . distinguished another cowering figure
looking at me furtively. The face was strongly distorted,
and the creature had a rope around its neck; the hands
trying constantly to secure the ends; at times also a finger
would move around the neck as if to loosen the rope. The
figure looked at me with eyes of terror starting from the
head, but not a word would cross the lips. It was plain I
must make the beginning.

"The light is decreasing,. . . . I fear we shall be quite
in the dark presently. Yes. How long will it last? How
should I know? It may be some hours, it may be a hundred
years. . . . It is always long, frightfully long.

"But it is quite certain that daylight *will* appear. If you
call that daylight which we used to call dusk upon earth;
we never get more. . . . I see you are a new-comer here."

"Yes quite new; I died but lately; a natural death.". . . .
The distorted face looked at me with a horrible grimace,
and there was silence. . . . The specter resumed ere long:
"It is hard to be doomed to carry one's life in one's hands.
There is no rest for me anywhere; I am forever trying
to escape; there is not a creature but wants to hang me.
Indeed you are capable of doing it yourself. I see it in
your eyes. . . . Do you see the ends of this rope? It is my
one aim to prevent people from getting hold of them, for
if once they succeed I shall be hanged in a jiffy. . . . It is
but foolishness and imagination I know;. . . . but I am utterly helpless, and whenever this foolish fear possesses me
afresh, I must run, – run as though I had a thousand lives
to lose.". . . . I made some movement with the arm nearest
my wretched neighbor. Evidently he imagined I was for
seizing the rope the ends of which he was tightly grasping,
and like a flash of lightning he vanished from my side.

The light decreased, until at last it was the mere ghost of
a radiance; it was plain I should find myself in utter darkness ere long. . . . darkness here is so dense, so heavy, it
oppresses poor souls as with the weight of centuries. . . . The

Bible calls it *"the outer darkness."*. . . . Terrible truth!
that the torments of hell should consist in an awful con-
trast—cold without and a consuming fire within. . . . There
burned within me the quenchless torment of sin and sinful
desire. . . . If conscience,—while on earth—at times made
some effort to be heard, the voice was so gentle that I never
hesitated to disregard it. . . .

You must know, then that each wretched being here is
moved by irresistible impulse to imitate his life on earth.
Passion and wrongful desires rule here as they do on the
earth, only the more horribly, being void of substance. . . .
No matter how deeply conscious we are of the vanity of
our doings,—no matter how we loathe them,—they have
come to be our masters; we are driven, helplessly driven,
to be forever trying to be what we were on earth. . . . There
is no sense left to gratify; reality has vanished; the greed
only remains.

GEOGRAPHY OF HELL:

Hell has its own geography. . . . no one can tell how far
its realm extends. . . . In the direction of the pale light that
increases and decreases alternately, there is a great gulf,
a fathomless abyss, separating Hell from Paradise. It is
Paradise whence that radiance proceeds. . . . and from the
abyss, apparently dead darkness gushes forth, repressing
the faint far-off light of heaven. . . . At times, a cataract of
light bursts forth victoriously, overflowing from the heart
of glory. Hell stands dazzled, struck to the core. . . . and it
is not only Paradise that we see but the blessed ones who
dwell there. . . . It is only by pushing toward and absorbing
that light that there is any hope of redemption."[2]

From another authoritative source we recount more vivid
descriptions of the various aspects of the regions of the Hell-
worlds which confirm that already given. These are the
experiences of those who, by their way of living on this earth-
plane, have built for themselves a "house of bondage" and

---

[2] For further details see *Letters from Hell*, Thisted.

"robes of sorrow" for the spirit-world, until such time as they are able to work out their own redemption by the recognition and acceptance of the love and power of God.

OTHER EXPERIENCES:

We receive the following from a discarnate spirit:[3] Whilst in England, the writer received from an unknown spirit the first experiences of this spirit in the spirit-world. He said that he found himself, with a number of others, in utter darkness, cold, hungry and most miserable. . . . In endeavoring to advance he and his companions found their progress obstructed by a massive and lofty wall. They felt along it to discover some door or passage through it, but could find none, though they continued their search to a great distance. At length, in despair, they shouted to make someone hear them, but for a long time received no answer, but a dreary and hollow echo. All else was silent, dead, a vacancy, and a most terrible negation.

Then they burst into cries of despair and desperation, when at length a voice demanded who they were and what they wanted. They replied that they were newly disembodied spirits, who were perishing with cold, starvation and nakedness. The response was, "You lived selfish lives,—lived for yourselves, while on earth. You felt no thankfulness to God, nor did you ever cherish in your hearts true love for your fellowmen. As you were an adamantine wall to humanity, an adamantine wall now rises inexorably before you, cutting off all admission to more favorable regions."

This terrible announcement struck them down like dead men. They bewailed themselves bitterly, and cried for mercy and pardon, and at length a voice exclaimed. "Arise" and a strong hand was put forth from the darkness, and the apparently impassable wall gave way to that mighty hand, and they found themselves in a dusky, as it were, Cimmerian meadow where friendly beings fed and clothed them and told them

---

[3] *Immortality*, Peebles, 111-119.

that now they were on the open highway to the pilgrimage of eternity, and must advance, grow purer and enjoy according to their own exertions to the obedience to their spiritual guides, to the prayerful love they exercised to the great Father, to the Law of Christ, and to the love of their neighbor. (Excerpts from *Immortality*, Peebles, 111-112.)

The lament of John Jacob Astor from the spirit world through the mediumship of Mrs. Conent:

"Gold is the strongest tie which binds men to earth, and if I were on earth again I would not be the owner of gold. I would rather take the chance of the beggar than that of the rich man. I would rather be cradled in sorrow on earth, for then I would better appreciate the joys of heaven. And as all men sin, so all men must be punished; I had rather receive my punishment on earth than in the land where we all hope for happiness. Yes, Yes, I would rather be a Lazarus—much rather; and could I again be transported to earth, could I again animate a material form, I would pray that God would give me the surroundings of a Lazarus rather than the surroundings of a rich man. When the rich man finds death at his door, he fears to leave his apparently real happiness for the imaginary—for that he knows nothing of. But when the poor man dies he says, 'I have nothing here to bind me, my chance is equally good in the land of the spirits.'. . . . All things that went up to make my sum of happiness on earth, are denied me in heaven; I partake not of its glories, for each individual forms his own heaven and his own hell. Heaven may be within me, above me, around me, and yet not of me. I may not be happy though others may be happy around me. How long I am to remain so I do not know. I know however, that he who judges righteously will not judge me harshly."[4]

The personal experiences of Aaron Knight, given from the spirit world:

"Although my father was a prominent churchman, and my brother, the Rev. James Knight, an English clergyman, I was

---

[4] *Immortality*, Peebles, 113-114.

a materialist and given to intoxicating liquors. Coming to consciousness in spirit life, I was at first inclined to doubt my existence; at least I could not realize that my body was dead. . . . I saw my body buried, which when done, the attending spirits left me to myself—left me alone.

"The atmosphere was dark hued and hazy. . . . I said to myself, "How strange, I see no God, no devil, no heaven, no hell,—and yet I exist. But oh! so lonely!' All learn in our life, if not in yours, that penalties, like shadows, follow us each and all, and none can get away from themselves. . . . After thinking intently upon some of the rollicking associates who passed to spirit-life before me, they were attracted to me by the psychic law of sympathy, and I joined them in their haunts, and engaged in their frivolous pursuits. My spirit-world at this time was my earth-world. . . . and my affections and thoughts continued on earthly things. My mind status and tendency of mind barred me away from the heavens. . . . My home was in the hells, but they were hells not entirely devoid of an inferior kind of pleasure. . . .

"Long weary years rolled away before I made any perceptible progress. . . . Remorse often stung me. I did not find complete rest. Some in states lower than mine had suffered intense anguish for long periods. They were wilful in their blindness. Their environments,—dark wastes, barren fields, dismal swamps, gloomy dens and caves of horror,— accorded fully with their internal desires and motives. . . .

"In the transition to a higher state of happiness, I was aided by my brother the clergyman. . . . I was dissatisfied with my associates, and while apart by myself praying, I saw in the distance a star. Reverently continuing my soul aspirations, the star seemed to approach nearer, expanding until it actually enveloped me in a halo of brightness, and out of this resplendent brightness, there came to me my brother. . . . I begged permission to go home, to his home in the heavens at once. . . . 'No,' he replied. "You can only come to our heavenly world when prepared. . . . Go directly to your old

associates as a teacher. . . . Aid and encourage them. . . .
and in blessing them you will be thrice blessed.' Often
from this onward did my brother come to me, and thus
aided by him and other noble teachers, I rapidly unfolded
until my surroundings are now divinely beautiful, and I
am permitted to minister to mortals.[5]

BLACK SPOTS:

"I approached one of these black spots and there, in a
miserable hovel, was a human being. He was ghastly, thin,
haggard—almost a skeleton. He knew no means of escape
from that dark habitation, where he was all alone. The most
violent of human passions were raging in him, and he was
walking back and forth like a chained tiger. . . .

"There was a little light in that habitation of his, but it
was an awful one. It was the red, flame-like light of his own
eyes. They were open and staring like burning coals, with
a black spot in their center, and were constantly straining
to see something,—the darkness was so horrible to him!
He had no companion but his own hatred and the memory
of his evil past.

"He paused once in a while in his walk, raising his
clenched hands above his head, and cursed his Maker that
ever He had created him. He cursed also the false teachers
who had pretended to tell him the consequences of a life of
sin, and yet knew so little of them. They had told him of a
hell of fire and brimstone only, and he knew that when he
died, casting off his material garb, such a hell could have
no effect on him. . . . Now waking to the reality of a hell
far worse than had ever been painted to him, he cursed
God and man that he had been left alone to dare its torments,—that he had been left in ignorance of what must
follow the indulgence of the material passions, to which
he had given up his whole life.

"If you had seen the agony that was painted on his face,
the despair and hatred that spoke in every lineament, the des-

---

[5] *Immortality*, Peebles, 87.

perate passion that swelled every muscle, and the horrible fear that stole over him of what further might ensue. . . . you would have shuddered and recoiled from the sight. . . . And what aggravated all this suffering was his ignorance that there was any redemption for him, and the belief that it was forever.

"He clasped his hands over his head in a gesture of mute despair, and standing thus for a few minutes he cried, 'Oh for annihilation!'. . . . If you could have heard the tone in which that imprecation was uttered, you could have formed an idea of the torments of the damned. . . . groveling in the dirt and writhing in agony, he howled like the most furious maniac that bedlam's worst cell ever saw. At length from sheer exhaustion he was still. . . . and, now, as he lay there prostrate and exhausted, solitary and in utter darkness, all the evil deeds of his life chased each other through his memory. . . . faithfully performing their terrible duty of retribution."[6]

Exploration of the hells by another spirit from the Higher Planes, gives us the following.

"The spirit-world, almost measureless in extent, has actual localities, as well as conditions, where sympathizing spirits meet. A higher spirit may visit the lower spheres, but the reverse is impossible. . . .

"Turning our attention to what is before us, we see in the widened distance, a misty darkness, and as we descend in an opposite direction from which we came, the darkness becomes more and more intensified. There is no vegetation, no sparkling rivers nor smiling lakes. As we pass on. . . . rising and crossing a range of hills, the harsh cries and the hoarse agonies that appall the soul, reveal the fact that we are in the neighborhood of dark and undeveloped spirits.

"We stand for a moment to mature plans for the thorough investigation of these cities of strife. . . . We each take a separate path. . . . the darkness fading into a lurid, dusky,

---

[6] *Immortality*, Peebles, 114 -115.

phosphorescent light, until we come to a huge cavern, around which are fierce reptiles, crawling lizards and slimy serpents, winding around each other as though in fond embrace. In the atmosphere are vultures, black and dismal — everything is terribly repulsive!. . . .

"We come to the conclusion that these fierce, loathsome and horrid creatures are the natural outbursts of just such dismal localities as this. . . .

CITY OF STRIFE:

"We discover a capacious, vault-like room, where reside two women and a man. Inquiring, we are informed that the two women in a quarrel about the man. . . . had, while on earth, murdered each other, one dying immediately and the other living a few days to rave in anger. The vile man soon after committed suicide! In malice, hate and strife they had lived on earth, and dying in strife, they were born into the spirit world; hence their home is in the City of Strife. And, as if to remind them of their past deeds, pictured streams of blood, seemingly roll down the sides of the deep black walls, of their dismal abode.

"Relating the sad story to us, they occasionally quarrel, accusing each other, and moaning in spirit; and as they do this, the reptiles and animals, so demon-like without, mock them, and ghastly bat-like creatures screech in dismal discords that echo through the cave-chambers. Here these persons are doomed to remain, until by punishment, by penance, by repentance and active deeds of reparation, they shall make amends for the past.

"Leaving the cavern by its only entrance, we find ourselves once more in the more free but impure atmosphere. . . . We come upon a cluster of wretched huts. Their exteriors are coarse and painful to behold, and their interiors are in perfect correspondence. Insects and lizards are also here, and the denizens of the air are pouring out their jarring discords. The

occupants of these squalid homes are of the same quar-
relsome nature, as the one we have just left. The *City of
Strife* is justly named."[7]

HORRORS CAMP:

"Travelling on our winding way over some barren
hills, whose frowning summits intercept the light from
the brighter scenes, is Horror's Camp! Its dwellers are
numerous, and principally those who have died in drunken
fits, or have come to these shores in some other vehicle of
crime and sin. Not that they merely *died* in any particular
passion, but, having lived lives of licentiousness and vice,
driving far away the light of virtue, they entered spirit-life
in this impure state.

"It is really touching enough to melt the heart of the
stoutest, to observe their furrowed brows, glaring eyes,
straggling hair, and boney, sinewy frames, half covered
in scarlet garments. We observe that some of them gaze
intently upon the dark and dismal walls, without removing
their eyes from the serpent-charmed spot. The scenes of
their past lives are in their most disgusting features, floating before their vision and playing upon the walls. They are
horrified at the sight of their own misdeeds, and they cry
out occasionally in wailing choruses. . . . Sometimes they
vary this monotony by endeavoring to relieve their earthly
lusts; but being unable, they are mortified and shocked
with horror, and then resort to new orgies, hoping to realize some carnal delight. It is surprising to hear how some
will talk to their comrades about virtue. . . . To listen to
their talk some of them on earth have lived exemplary
and virtuous lives; yet they are the most depraved and
degraded of any. These more talkative characters will draw
plans. . . . that they may return to earth, that they may influence mortals and in this way gratify their propensities. . . .
the affair generally ends in a quarrel. And so here they
remain, poor vice-strung souls; horror-bound they sigh in

---

[7] Immortality, Peebles, 117-118.

restless suspense, daily exhibiting their contempt for the laws of man and God."[8]

THE HELLS MITIGATED:

"Three of us resolve to continue in one of these hells and watch the method of reaching and redeeming these people of the lower spheres. We select the case of a man who has been in darkness some time, yet seems possessed of some good tendencies. His abode is in a den beneath an over-hanging cliff, dimly illumined by a ghastly light. It should be remembered that the Divine Light partially illuminates, and the Divine Life,—by the law of the influx—flows into all spheres.

"Unseen by this person we watch him carefully, notic-ing every act and listening to every ejaculation. In this way we learn that in a revengeful quarrel with his brother, while on earth, he inflicted upon himself a fatal wound, and was borne to this dark place. He gravitated to his own place just as naturally as a stone falls to the earth. Here he indulges at times in expressions of anger, revenge, and terrible threats. Upon one occasion after these wild rav-ings, we see him sitting upon a cliff and sadder than usual, doubtless thinking of his misspent and vicious life. He cries out in the fullness of his soul. 'What! am I here for trying to slay my brother? O heaven! I've been mad.' and the tears such as only spirits can shed, stream down his face, upon the crystal rocks beneath. And while thus weeping, the vapor of his thoughts gather round him, in-filling his demon home with sorrow. Soon we begin to witness his gradual transformation.

"The rocks disappear; the fierce howlings in the air are hushed, and this seemingly lost soul, angel-guided, finds him-self in a dismal cellar, in one of the filthy streets of Liverpool, England. Here on a pallet of straw without the comforts of home, lies his brother almost dying! Remembering at once his past unkindnesses, the scene touches his soul's vi-tals. He weeps; and tenderly bending over the sickly form,

---

[8] *Immortality*, Peebles, 117-118.

he prays. 'Oh God and O father and mother,—angels now—forgive my past sins, and make me better in the future; for Christ's sake. Amen.'

"His tears, his earnest prayers, draw others to him though he is not aware of their presence. They give him strength, and he imparts it in love waves of magnetism to his deeply wronged and suffering brother. This continues for months the sick man growing weaker and fainter. But all this time the good thoughts of each enlist the interests of higher spirits, while the two brothers, by their thoughts and deeds of kindness, build a home in the better land. The last we witness is when earth yields up its claim, and the released brother, leaving the body, is borne in slumbers sweet, to the abode awaiting him, by the brother, now more angel made. As time passes on the flowers grow, the trees sigh, the streams ripple, and the birds sing sweetly in adjoining groves; for no inharmony, no sloth abides in that home. And so in blessing another the blessing is returned. . . . Here you may ask, even though our motive was good, how could we leave our sunbright abodes and tarry in the murky atmosphere of the hells? Be our answer. Spirits project the atmosphere or aural emanation in which they live and move. When descending into the hells, this personal atmosphere becomes a protective envelope, being positive to the general as well as to the individual atmospheres of lower spheres. But if one attempts to ascend from a lower to a higher sphere his characteristic emanations are negative to the aromatic flames, which then become to him a consuming fire."[9]

"In regard to suicide, I can only say, that if men knew what waits those who go out by their own hand, they would rather remain with the evil that they know."[10]

In reading the above descriptions, the basic comforting thought is, that even in the blackest depths of hell there is always the possibility and availability of reform and redemp-

---

[9] *Immortality*, Peebles.
[10] *Letters From a Living Dead Man*, Barker.

tion, whenever the soul desires or seeks it. In other words, since the love of God is all powerful and everlasting, it is always available to those who seek it. There is no *eternal* damnation, but *for only such time as the soul condemns itself by its refusal to respond to the redemptive power of God's love*. In these present days, when men are so gladly hearing afresh that "in Him is no darkness at all" is it believable that God could have created any man if he knew that he must live in torture through all Eternity; and that His hatred toward evil cannot be expressed by injustice,—itself the arc essence of evil? For certainly it would be nothing less than injustice to punish *infinitely* what was *finitely* committed; no sinner being capable of understanding the enormity of what he does.

Chapter XXIV

LETTERS FROM HEAVEN

In 1909 the mother of the Rev. G. Dale Owen, Vicar of Oxford, Lancaster, England, passed over to the other side. In 1913 his wife developed the power of automatic writing, and through her he received the request that he himself would sit quietly, with a pencil in his hand, and take down any thoughts which seemed to come into his mind, projected there by any external personality, and not consequent on the exercise of his own mentality. From these writings developed the four volumes comprising *The Life Beyond the Veil*, describing life in the astral, from the first of which *The Lowlands of Heaven*, we requote in this chapter, as follows:

"A few words of the conditions we found when we arrived here,—the conditions that is of those who pass over here when they first arrive. They are not all of the same spiritual degree of development, of course, and therefore require different treatment. Many, as you know, do not seem to realize the fact that they are what they would call dead, because they find themselves alive and with a body, and their previous vague notions of the after-death state are not by any means lightly thrown away.

"The first thing to do then with such as these is to help them to realize that they are no more in the earth life, and to do this we employ many methods. One is to ask them whether they remember some friend or relative, and when they reply that they do so but that he is dead, we try to enable them to see this particular spirit who appearing alive should convince the doubter that he had really passed over. This is not always the case for the ingrained fallacies are obstinate, and so we try another method.

"We take him to some scene on earth with which he is familiar and show him those left behind and the difference in his state and theirs. If this should fail, then we bring to his recollection the last experiences he underwent before passing, and gradually lead up to the time when he fell asleep. Then we try to connect up that moment with his awakening here.

"All of these endeavors often fail,—more often than you would imagine—for character is builded up year by year, and the ideas which go to help in this building, become finally imbedded in his character. Also, we have to be very careful not to overtax him, or it would delay his enlightenment. Sometimes however, in the case of those who are more enlightened, they realize immediately that they are passed into the spirit land, and then our work is easy. I fear many of you when you come over here will be shocked to see how very natural all things are, even if more beautiful than on earth. So many expect to find a vague, shadowy world over here, totally diverse from earth in every way. And yet come to think of it, and with common sense, what good would such a world be to us? It would mean not a gradual progress for us but a vast leap, and that is not the way of God.

"Many things here when we first arrive are certainly different from those of the old life, but not so different as to make us feel dumbfounded by their strangeness. Indeed those who came over after living an unprogressive life on earth, find themselves in spheres of so gross a character, as to be to them, indistinguishable from earth itself. That is one of the reasons they are not able to realize that they have changed their state. As you progress through the lower spheres into the higher, this grossness gradually gives place to more rare conditions, and the higher you go the more sublimated the environment. But few if any, pass into those spheres where no trace of earth is seen, or no likeness to the earth-life. I doubt if as a rule any do, but of this I must speak dogmatically, for I have not myself reached, or even visited a sphere where there is no likeness to God's beautiful earth. Earth is but one *manifestation further outward* from our own spheres, and in tune with us and our present environment in many very intimate ways. Were it not thus we would not be communing with you at this moment.

"It would probably be utterly absurd to many to be told that here we have real solid houses and streets; mountains and trees and animals and birds, and that animals are not here for ornament alone, but also for use; and that horses, oxen and other animals are put to use. But they seem to enjoy their work which makes one glad to watch them.

"As we gaze out over the wide planes and valleys of the Heavenly Land, we are scarce able to remember the effect of the atmosphere of earth as it had relation to our vision of terrestrial things. But we do remember certain qualities which are here absent. Distance is not obscured, for instance; it fades away. Trees and plants do not appear for a season and then die, but bloom perpetually, and then when they are plucked, they are fresh for a long time, but they do not droop and wither. They too fade away into the atmosphere. This same atmosphere is not always white. It is not a mist and does not always obscure, but bathes all things in its golden radiance without invading the various colors themselves. In other places it is a faint pink or blue and every region has its own peculiar tint, or sense of color, according to the nature of the people and their employment and bent of mind.

"One of the things that matter here is that due proportion be meted out between wisdom and love. These are not contrary the one to the other, but are two great phases of one principle. For love is to wisdom as the tree is to the leaves, and if love actuate and wisdom breathe then the fruit is healthy and sound.

"Light is not always conducive to peace, but in its passage creates a series of vibrations which often bring destruction to those species of living creatures which are not fashioned to survive in the light of the sun. Let them go . . . . and your eyes will become accustomed to the greater light, the beauty of the Love of God, the very intensity of which, blended as it is with infinite wisdom, is perplexing to those who are not altogether in the light.

"Our home over here is very bright and beautiful, and others from the higher spheres continually descend and visit us to cheer us on the upward way. These higher companions are visible to the others when they wish to be, and according to the development of those they visit.

PASSING SCENES:

"We will tell you of a scene which we witnessed not long ago. . . . We were told that a ceremony was about to take place in a certain wide plain not far from our home, at which we might be present. It was the ceremony of initiation of one who had passed the gate of what we will call *prejudice*,—that is prejudice against those who are not of his particular way of learning,—and who was about to go forth into a wider and fuller sphere of usefulness.

"We found a great many people arriving from all directions. Some came on foot, others in horse-drawn chariots, without reins and guided by mind power. Others came by aerial flight without the use of wings. We began to sing and although no instrument was visible, yet instrumental music blended with our singing and became one with it. It was very beautiful and served both as a reward to those who had earned it, and a spur to those who had still to tread the path. The music proceeded from a temple grove outside the circle. . . . and seemed to be a part of the atmosphere.

"When they had all gathered, a circle was made, and one stepped out, the one who was to be initiated, and he wore a robe of orange color. . . . not like the color as you know it;—none of our colors are. . . .

AN EXPERIENCE:

"The initiate took me by the hand and led me away. We walked for a little time and then I felt my feet leave the ground and we went through the air. I was not afraid for his strength was given to me. . . . we descended in a city where I had not been before. . . . I soon made out that we were in a garden surrounding a large building. . . . The building seemed all of one piece of material of different hues, pink and blue and red and yellow, which shone like gold but softly. Up the steps we went, and at the great doorway without any door to it, we met a very beautiful lady, stately but not proud. She was the Angel of the House of Sorrow. . . . The sorrow is not of those who dwell there but is the lot of those to whom they minister. The sorrowful ones are those on earth, and it is the business of the residents of this House to send to them vibrations which have the effect of neutralizing the vibrations of the sorrowful hearts on earth. You must understand that here we must get at the bottom of things, and learn the cause of things, and that it is a very deep study. Our occupation varies according to the needs of those to whom we minister. It is very varied but directed to the uplift of those who are still in earth-life. This then is my present phase of service, and a very happy one it promises to be. But I have only just begun to understand the prayers which are brought to us here and registered, and the sighs of those in trouble we hear,—or rather they too are registered,—and we feel or see them as it were, and send out our own vibrations in answer. As the effects are also registered back again to us, I know the amount of comfort and help we send.

"We were led back into the grounds which surrounded the house, and there we found gardeners at work, tending the flowers and fruit trees, and doing the general work of a garden. He took us some distance along the walks winding here and there, and through plantations of trees and shrubs, where birds were singing and small, pretty, furry animals played

here and there. At length we came to a stream and by it
stood a stone arbor, which reminded me of a miniature
temple of Egypt.

"The grounds were very extensive and all have a kind
of relationship to the buildings,—a kind of responsiveness.
For instance the trees are true trees, and grow much as trees
do on earth, but they have a kind of responsiveness to the
buildings; and different kinds of trees respond more to one
house than to the others, and help the effect and work for
which that particular house was raised. So it is with the
grouping of trees in the groves, and the bordering flower-
beds of the paths, and the arrangement of the streams and
falls which are found in different parts of the grounds, all
these things have been brought out with marvelous wisdom, and the effect produced is very beautiful.

"These houses have not been raised merely mechani-
cally, but are the outcome,—growth if you will,—of the
action of the will of those high in rank in these realms; and
so they are of very powerful creative wills.

LIFE OF CHILDREN:

"A certain building is reserved for the children who
are still-born and have never breathed the atmosphere of
earth. These children are different from those who have
been born alive and have breathed the earth atmosphere,
even if only for a very few minutes, and for this reason they
require a different treatment, and are able sooner to imbibe
the knowledge of these spheres. So they are sent to some
special homes by themselves, where they are trained until
they have progressed in mind and statue to such a degree,
that they are able to begin their new course of knowledge.
Then, having become strong in heavenly purity and wisdom, they are taken in hand by those teachers who are in
touch with the earth itself, and they are taught what they
have not been able to learn before.

"When young children come over here they are first
schooled in this life and then have to learn what experience

they have lacked on earth. The more training they have acquired in the earth life, the sooner they are sent to complete it. Those who are still-born have had no training at all. Nevertheless they are children of earth and as such they must return and acquire this training. Not until it is safe for them to do so however, and then under proper guardianship, until they are competent to go alone. . . . One who has lived a long and busy life on earth has less to learn of earth life when he comes over here, and so he can progress to other studies.

"There are regions where there are many institutions mostly devoted to the study of the best ways of helping those on earth who are in doubt and perplexity as to the problems which stretch out into the realms beyond.

OTHER SCENES:

"Our guides led us to one of those plains of Heaven where Manifestations from the higher Heavens are sometimes given. The call goes forth and vast multitudes assemble, and then some of the glories of the highest spheres are manifested as well as it is possible in these lower realms. . . .

"We received a message a short time ago of the arrival of a sister at the *Bridge* who had come over from the farther side where lie the regions of gloom, and I and another were sent to conduct her to this Home. We went quickly and found our charge awaiting us. She was quite alone for her attendants had left her thus in order that she might profit by a quiet period of meditation and reflection, before beginning her further advance.

"When she opened her eyes she looked up at us for some time in an inquiring manner. I addressed her as 'sister' and at that word her eyes began to fill with tears, and she wept bitterly. . . .

" 'How do you know who or what I am" she said.

" 'We do not know *who* you are. . . . We do know that you were and are *always* a child of our Father, and so *always* our sister. What else you are lies with you. You are either one whose face is turned toward the Sunshine of His Presence, or one. . . . who will turn back across the Bridge.'

"She said, 'I dare not, it is all too horrible back there'. Then I told her that for the present she must try to forget those experiences, until we had helped her. . . . There is only one way onward, nothing can be glossed over. Everything must be viewed and understood for what it is,—every act and word to the present time,—God's justice acknowledged and God's love through all,—and that is the only onward and upward way.

"We told her all about the home to which she was being led. . . . and in the midst of it all she stopped suddenly and said that she felt she could go no further, that she was afraid.

"'But,' I urged, 'You must choose for you cannot remain where you are. And you will come the upward way—will you not? And we will lend you a sister's hand, and give you a sister's love to help you on the way. . . . In the midst of our conversation she stopped suddenly and said she felt again that she could go on no further. 'Why?' we inquired, 'are you tired?' and she answered again 'No, afraid.'

"When we questioned her she told us the following: It seems that when the guardian at the other end of the bridge had heard her cry for help, far away in the gloom, he at once directed a ray of light in the direction and sent a messenger to help her. This spirit found her fainting by the side of a dark murky stream whose waters were foul and hot, and bore her to the Gatehouse at the Bridge. Here she was tended and revived, and brought forward across the Bridge, where we found her.

"Now it chanced that when the spirit worker had found her, she had felt a presence, but could not see anyone near. She therefore called aloud, 'May you be cursed if you touch me!' thinking it was one of her old tormenters and companions in wickedness. Then she remembered no more until she recovered her senses again in the Gatehouse. . . . She had cursed one of God's ministers, and she was afraid of the light because the words were evil. Truly she did not know whom she had cursed; but a curse is a curse, against whomsoever directed, and it lay upon her heart. . . . This was against one of her fellow workers of the realms of light and love and we saw that she would find no rest among us, and our services would little avail her, until that wrong had been righted. So back to the Bridge we went and right across it to the Gatehouse at the further end. There we found the spirit helper who had brought her to that place, and she asked and obtained forgiveness. Indeed he was awaiting us, for he was stronger than we and greater in wisdom, and he knew that she would compel herself to return. . . . When she saw the face of the one against whom she had sinned, and heard his words of love and forgiveness, it showed her for the first time that whatever she had to endure in the future, it would be sweet in the end, and each task done would earn its own blessing.

JUDGMENT:

"One of our poor sisters inquired of our Mother Angel, 'Where is the Judge, and when is the judgment to take place? I am trembling at the thought of it for I know my punishment will be a very dreadful one, and I would know the worst and get it over with.'

"To this the mother replied. 'My child your judgment will take place whenever you desire it, and I can tell by your own words that it has already begun. For you own that your past life is worthy of punishment and that is the first step in your judgment. As for the Judge, well, she is here; for *you yourself are judge* and will mete out to yourself your own punishment. You will do this of your own free-will by reviewing all the life you have lived, and as you bravely own up one sin after another so you will progress. Much of your punishment you have already inflicted upon yourself in the dark regions from which you have lately come. That punishment was indeed dreadful, but that is past and over, and what you have now to endure will be dreadful no longer. All dread should now be past. Painful, deeply painful I fear it will be, but all through you will feel that He is leading you, and this more and more as you go on in the right way.'

" 'But' persisted the inquirer, 'I am perplexed because I do not see the throne of the Great Judge, Who will reward some and punish others.'

" 'You will indeed some day see that throne, but not yet. The judgment you are thinking of is very different from what you imagine. But you should have no fear and as you progress you will learn more and understand more of God's great love.'

"That is what perplexes many who come over here. They expect to find all set ready for their dismissal from the Presence into torture, and cannot understand things as they are.

"Others who have cultivated a good opinion of their deserts are much disappointed when they are given a lowly place, sometimes a very lowly one, and not ushered immediately into the Presence of the Enthroned Christ to be hailed with His 'Well Done.' Oh! there are many surprises awaiting those who come over here, some of a very joyful kind and others the reverse.

DIFFICULTIES OF SPIRIT COMMUNICATORS:

"And now let us see if we can explain a difficulty which is perplexing many investigators into psychic matters. We mean the difficulty they have in understanding why we do not give them exact information which they desire about one thing or another which they have in their minds. You must try to realize that when we come down here to you, we are not in our proper element, but are hampered with limitations which are now strange to us. For instance we have to work according to the laws which are in vogue in the earth realm, or we could not make you understand what we wish to do or say. Then we often find that when anyone has his mind fixed on some particular person whom he wishes to see or hear, or some special matter about which he wishes to inquire, we are limited by the straightened means at our disposal. Other reservoirs of power in that inquirer are closed, and those only are open to us which he himself has willed to be opened. And these are frequently not enough for us to work with.

"Then again, the activity of his will meets the activity of ours midway as it were, and there is a clash, and the result is either confusion or nil. It is nearly always better to allow us to work in our own way, trustfully, and afterwards to examine critically what we manage to get through. If information on any particular point is desired, let that point be in your minds at times as you go about your daily occupation. We shall see it and take account of it, and if it is possible and useful and lawful, we shall find opportunity and means sooner or later to answer it. If you ask a question while we are with you, manifesting in one way or another, do not demand but just put your thoughts before us, and then leave it to us to do what we can. Do not insist. You may be sure that, as our desire is to help we will do all we can. . . .

"The power we use is best described as magnetism, and by this the vibrations of our minds are directed to your own. Your hand being placed against your head serves as a kind of magnet and reservoir in one and helps us. . . .

"In our life in the summerland we endeavor to help both those who come over to us and also their friends still on earth. Indeed the two phases of service are inseparable, for those who pass over here are often much distressed, and so are unable to progress, until they know that those they left behind are being helped from this side. So we often make excursions to the Earth plane for this reason.

NAMES:

"What's in a name? Well from our point of view and, that also of the ancient wisdom of Egypt, based on data obtained on this side of the veil, there is a great deal in a name. Even in the repetition of some names there is actual power and sometimes peril. That we know now as we did not when we were on earth. And so we here acquire a reverence for the entity 'The Name' which to you would probably seem foolish. Nevertheless it is partly for this reason that names do not come through to you so plentifully, as many rather feeble investigators would wish.

"Also the mere utterance and transmission of some of these names is, when we are in this earth region, a matter of more difficulty than you would perhaps deem. It is a subject however which is hard to explain to you, and only one which you will be able to understand when you have become more familiar with the fourth dimension which obtains here,—which term also we use for want of a better. We will just refer you to two or three instances and there leave the matter.

"One is the giving to Moses of the Name of the great Officer of the Supreme, Who visited him. Moses asked for that name and got it,—and neither he nor anyone else to his day has been able to say what it means.

"Then the lesser Angel who came to Jacob. Jacob asked for his name and it was refused him. The Angels who came to Abraham and to others in the Old Testament, very seldom gave their names. Likewise in the New Testament, most of the Angels who came to minister to earth's denizens, are simply so called, and when the name is given, as in the case of Gabriel, it is little understood as to its significance.

OTHER MESSENGERS:

"We are spiritual ministers from another sphere, where your own friends and your mother have visited from time to time. . . . She and her friends come to us for instruction. We are glad to come,—and to know you,—at the request of your mother. Never imagine that we are troubled to come to this earth sphere, for although it does mean an experience of less brightness in environment, than is our usual lot; yet the privilege counterbalances that more and more. . . .

"We understand much that was not clear to us when we walked amidst the shadows on earth. And this we would say with all solemnity: let those who to-day amongst you are searching into the meaning of His Divinity and the relation of this to His Humanity, do so fearlessly and reverently. For such are guided more than they know from these realms. . . .

"Friend, we tell you, with this same fearlessness, and with great reverence also, that what goes by the name of orthodoxy among the Christians in the church on Earth, is not a true and fair presentation in many ways of the Truth as we have come to know it here. . . .

DREAMS:

"I was impressing a man who was investigating the laws of psychology in the matter of visions and dreams. He wanted to find out what was the cause of certain dreams being prophetic,—the connection between the dream itself and the incident which it foreshadowed. He applied to me and I told him that he must continue his investigations and use his own mind, and, if it were well it would be given to him to understand.

ZONES:

"When we said 'the Powers which watch over the world', we did not mean to localize these powers on one side of this planet, but to apply the all-enveloping watch which the heavenly powers keep about the sphere which is called Earth. These Powers are resident in the Zones of which the Earth itself is the center, and they lie in concentric circles around it. The inferior zones are those near the planet's surface, and progress in power and glory as the distance is increased. And yet, space must be enlarged in meaning when applied to these spheres; for distance has not the same obstructive sense to us as it has to you. . . . So we may for the sake of clarity, put it thus: The Earth is the center about which many spheres are, and is enclosed in all these spheres. And the residents in the Earth life are potentially in touch with all those spheres, and actually so in ratio to their altitude spiritually considered,—spiritually, because these spheres are spiritual and not material.[1]

"You will now have some idea of what prayer and aspiration and worship mean. They are the means of communion with the Creator, and His High and Holy Ones, Who,—to put it in a way that you will understand,—dwell in the highest or outmost of these spheres, and include within Himself and These all those zones within the highest Zone or Sphere."[2]

DEGREES IN SPIRIT LIFE:

In a report from another great writer we find the following message from the other side of the veil:

"When I passed to spirit life I entered into the fourth degree of happiness. Each degree is divided into what may be denominated fifteen compartments. I was too young of course to have known sin, but I was also too young to have advanced in spiritual progression. I am now in the fifth degree and hope very soon to enter the sixth with my mother.

"We have our homes, our houses, our fruits, birds, flowers, plants, trees, everything in fact, that you have on Earth, and as tangible to us as material things are to you. There is no sorrow in our home. It is only when we witness the sorrow and suffering of Earth's inhabitants, that we are unhappy. . . . Everytime we are permitted to make ourselves known,—to our Earth friends,—we are advanced. . . . Our home was not made by hands but by pure thoughts, and good actions expressed in the earthly life."[3]

From another noted spirit communicator we find that life goes on, on the other side much the same as it does on our Earth plane.

---

[1] For further details see *Realms of the Living Dead*, Curtiss.
[2] For further details see, *The Lowlands of Heaven*, Owen.
[3] *Immortality*, Peebles, 194.

"Often I have told you that this world is, almost to completeness, the counterpart of Earth and its inhabitants. Consequently social and domestic relations ate very similar. Wedded bliss is numbered among the numerous joys that abound in the spiritual world. But marriages, in the spheres, are not based upon the ceremonial, nor are they for the purpose of procreation and self-gratification, but rather for social interblendings, and the quickening of the Spiritual activities. . . . On earth I was called a bachelor, and I retain such yet if by it is meant individualized singleness, relative to connubial life. Still I consider all things from the minutest monads to the most royal soul— angels—to be dual; and I believe men and women to be the two hemispheres of the sphere, and as positives and negatives, corresponding to wisdom and love, they were designed for sacred unions. If these are based on selfishness, they necessarily terminate sooner or later; but if true and well fitted, the spiritual dominating when on Earth, they continue on in our world of spirits. Ancient seers and sages however, who have summered many thousand years in the heavens, assure me that, progressively inclined spirits so unfold, so approximate the Divine, that ultimately their loves become *universal*, the love of each flowing out to all, as the sun shines upon all, and as God's life and love flow into all immortal intelligences."[4]

As we have explained in another chapter, the following excerpts from letters, came to the author Elsa Barker, from a discarnate friend, Judge Hatch, who used the method of automatic writing for the purpose of communication.

"I should be very sorry if the reading of these letters of mine should cause foolish and unthinking people to go spirit-hunting, inviting into their human sphere the irresponsible and often, lying elemental spirits. Tell them not to do it.

"Do not be too sure that the entity which raps on your table or your cupboard, is the spirit of your deceased uncle or grandfather. It may be a blind and *very desirous* entity,

---

[4] *Immortality*, Peebles, 92.

an eager consciousness trying to use you to hasten its own evolution; trying to get into you or through you so as to enjoy the Earth and the coarser vibrations of the Earth. It may not be able to harm you but on the other hand, it may do you no good.

"It is strange, but many persons seem to be in the regular orthodox heaven, singing in white robes with crowns on their heads, and with harps in their hands. There is a region which outsiders call the 'heaven country.' There is also, they tell me, a fiery hell, with, at least the *smell* of brimstone; but I have not been there yet. Some day when I feel strong I will look in. . . .

"Notwithstanding the companionship I have here, I sometimes regret my failure in holding onto the world. But regrets have less weight on this side,—like our bodies. Do not fear death but stay on Earth as long as you can.

"You need to take certain precautions to protect yourself from those who press around me. You have only to *lay a spell* upon yourself night and morning. Nothing can get through that wall,—nothing which you forbid your soul to entertain. . . . You have nothing to fear if you protect yourself.

"The teacher showed me how to create garments such as I desired; to fix the pattern and shape clearly in my mind, to visualize it, and then by *power* to desire to draw the subtle matter of the thought-world round the pattern, so as to actually form the garment.

"Those people who think of their departed friends as being all-wise, how disappointed they would be if they would know that the life on this side is only an extension of the life on Earth. If the thoughts and desires there have been only for pleasures, the thoughts and desires here are likely to be the same.

"Many times I have seen men and women lying in a state of unconsciousness more profound than the deepest sleep, their faces expressionless and uninteresting. . . . I tried to

awaken one or two of them, but was not successfull. . . .
I returned and found them lying in the same lethargy. . . .
To my question as to *why*, the Teacher replied. 'They are
those who in the earth-life denied the immortality of the
soul after death. . . .'

" 'And will they never awaken?'

" 'Yes, perhaps centuries, perhaps ages hence, when
the irresistible law of rhythm shall draw them out of their
sleep into incarnation, for the law of rebirth is one with
the law of rhythm, I said.

" 'Perhaps you with your greater power and knowledge
could succeed where I have failed. . . . Will you not try to
awaken this man?

" 'You know not what you ask', he replied. . . . 'In order
to counteract the law which holds him in sleep, the law of
the spell he laid upon his own soul when he went out of life
demanding unconsciousness and annihilation. . . . in order
to counteract *that* law I should have to put into operation a
law still stronger. *Will*. . . . the potency of the will. . . . Will
you tell me your reason for asking me to do this?'. . . . I
admitted that it was scientific curiosity on my part.

" 'In that case,' the teacher said, 'I am justified in using
him as a demonstration of the power of the trained will.'

" ' As far as he is concerned he is not worth the amount
of energy as will be necessary to arouse him from this
spell which he laid upon himself ages ago. . . . I see in the
pale light around the recumbent form, many pictures of
the soul's past. I see that he not only denied immortality
of the soul's consciousness, but he taught that doctrine of
death to other men.

"He then awakened him, but by what method and by
what words, I am not permitted to tell you.

" 'Where am I?' said the man, when he had awakened.

" ' You are where you always have been and always will
be, in eternity,' said the teacher.

" ' And who are you.'

" 'I am one who knows the workings of the Law. . . . of rhythm, which drives the soul in and out of gross matter,. . . . and the consciousness of man into sleeping and waking. . . .'

"This man by his misdirected will had been temporarily able to transcend the law of immortality, even as the Teacher, by his wisely directed will, transcended the mortal in himself! My soul sang within me at this glimpse of the godlike possibilities of the human mind.

"When one leaves the earth full of a great affection, and when the earthly loved one does not forget, the tie can hold for many years unweakened. You on earth have forgotten so much of what you have learned here, that you do not realize how your forgetfulness of us can throw us back upon ourselves.

REINCARNATION:

"Many souls stay out here until they are as tired of this world as they were formerly tired of the Earth, and then are driven back, half unconsciously, by the irresistible force of rhythm. These are the unadvanced souls who are drawn to their parents by the force of karma, and not by choice. Until you are willing to go in and out of dense matter, you will never learn to transcend matter. There are those who can stay in and out at will, and relatively speaking, as long as they choose. Those who do not believe in rebirth cannot forever escape the rhythm of rebirth; but they hold to their belief until the tide of rhythm sweeps them along with it and forces them into gross matter again, into which they go quite unprepared, carrying with them almost no memory of their life out here. They carried out here the memory of their Earth life because they expected to carry it.

Many persons out here sink into a sort of subjective bliss, which makes them indifferent as to what is going on upon the Earth, or in the heavens.

"Some souls would go back almost at once which is a mistake. Unless one is young, and still has a store of unused energy saved over from the last life, in going back to the Earth too soon, one lacks the force of a strong rebound. In such cases they live out only the unfinished part of their former life span. . . ."

In speaking of these letters the author says; "The effect of these letters on me personally is to remove entirely any fear of death, which I may ever have had; to strengthen my belief in immortality; to make life beyond the grave as vital, as real as life here in the sunshine. If they can give to *even one other person* the same sense of exultant immortality which they have given to me I shall feel repaid for my labor."[5]

To sum up the truths told in these *Letters From Heaven*, we quote again from the message communicated to the Rev. G. Vale Owen, by the spiritual ministers from the spiritworld.

"Be sure, friend, and tell others who will hear it,—that this life which awaits you is not a mere bodiless dream in a twilight region, somewhere beyond the real and the actual. No! It is strenuous and intense this life of ours. It is filled with service and endeavors, crowned one after another, with success; of patient pressing onward, and of indomitable wills attuned each to the other, in comrade service for the Lord of Love, whose life we sense and insure; but whom we do not see, and whose home is too sublime for us to know.

"But we testify to you, friend, and to those who will think reverently of these things they cannot understand, that if wonder gives us pause time and time again, as we proceed, yet never do we lose that sense of a Presence whose breathing is of love, and Whose leading is as gentle as the mother's leading of her little child. So we, as you do, take His hand and do not fear; and the music of the spheres is around us as we go from glory to the glory beyond. . . .

---

[5] Letters From *A Living Dead Man*, Barker.

Personal Survival

Never faint nor grow weary of the road, for the mists are thinning as you proceed, and the light strengthens into the further light which issues onward into the unknown, which is never feared. So we tread gently and humbly. . . . amid the glories of the planets, and the heavens of suns and spheres, and of the Love of God."

Chapter XXV

CONCLUSION

"Spiritualism, with its rational regard for God as Spirit, pervading all life, and prayer as the key to inner understanding, must appeal to ever increasing numbers of earnest thinking people. We can hope that succeeding generations, will not then blame God for the misdeed of men, but will find the cause in themselves,—and the cure too."[1]

As we have said in the preface of this volume, *Personal Survival*, the particular aim is to bring comfort, solace and assurance to countless thousands, through the realization and understanding of all life, and particularly of the life which goes on after death. In this concluding chapter we will speak of Spiritualism in a general way, its attributes, its value to humanity, its use for individual growth, its place in the Great Plan, and also its pitfalls and dangers.

Spiritualism teaches anew the indestructibility of the human spirit. That in itself would be one of the greatest services in the years to come. When men realize that they cannot in fact destroy the human spirit, they may give up trying to kill the body through which it functions. And once that is accepted, we may have the sure foundation for a long period of peace. It is like a family reunion, for it is the end of grief and the end of not knowing.

Spiritualism teaches anew a great international service without regard to race, creed, class distinction or color of skin.

Many have come to the séance room with minds dark with

---

[1] 1 *Psychic News*, August, 1945.

grief, and a few words from beyond the veil have altered
their whole outlook.

Science changes its views on many things, and has to
rewrite its text books every few years, but the fundamen-
tals of Psychic Research remain the same. It continues to
progress, for the results of such investigations but confirm
and elaborate its earlier statements.

The conditions for spiritualistic achievement are simple;
first a still mind; second a readiness to face facts; third reasonable judgment through which all statements must pass
before they are accepted. You require no expert knowledge,
only a desire to know the truth.

One case of survival would be a mystery, and the starting point of a thousand legends. But when one is followed
by a million, then you have something which has to be
considered as a fundamental contribution to civilization.
The evidence of one case might well give rise to skepticism
or doubt, but the evidence of millions of cases constitutes
an avalanche which sweeps away all doubtful objections.

Principles of Spiritualism:

There are certain general principles or *truths* which
must be accepted and used as a working basis. First and
foremost of these is the truth that *no life dies*, but only the
form is changed from time to time, and this changing of
the form of life is what is usually called "death." As one
writer received this truth from the spirit world, "It is so that
I am changed;—so all we *dead* are changed; glorified with
our *own* immortality, even as you too will be glorified. We
have indeed 'gone on' beyond the comprehension of your
present Earth conceptions."[2]

One of the first principles of Spiritualism is that everyone
must find out and *know* the truth for himself. The evidences
of survival are available to anyone who with earnest sincerity, openmindedness and a willingness to seek and work, is

---

[2] *Unobstructed Universe*, White, 33.

willing to lay aside his prejudices and creed superstition, and open his mind to further enlightenment.

ACROSS THE CHASM:

From across the chasm of so-called death comes the following reassuring message:

"There are millions who yearn to reveal that love is deathless; that the grave has no power to touch those whom love has united forever.

"It is always our task to build more bridges across the chasm of death, to open new roads, to find more *instruments*, to encourage them to develop their *divine* gifts to the highest, to teach them to be unselfish, and unwearying in service, so that more and more may be brought within the orbit of that wonderous knowledge, which dispels darkness and fear, and brings light and confidence to those who did not possess them before.

"I have returned to teach certain truths, truths that I have learned, truths very elementary, very simple yet fundamental, for without these truths man does not know his place in the great Cosmic Scheme of life."[3]

UNIVERSAL PANACAEA:

"In this world the chief difficulty arises from the contest between the 'Haves' and the 'Have-nots,' which is the root of most of our envy, hatred and malice. But there is no need for this at all in the next stage, since anyone can secure whatever he chooses by concentrating upon it; thus he needs envy nobody.

"Money becomes entirely superfluous where there are no goods on sale. And the miser who once hugged his money bags may continue to hug them still in the beyond, and though full, they are now meaningless. *The only true wealth consists in character; for even knowledge such as we gain here is often of little use in the next stage, and a kindly*

---

[3] A message from Silver Birch, *Psychic News*, Feb. 9th, 1946.

disposition and a heart of gold are far more really riches.
"But there are no compulsions. If we want to advance we
may. If we want to stagnate we are allowed to do so. Yet
after a time it is the common experience. . . . that souls
find their happiness only in growth and steady progress."[4]

WORKING PRINCIPLE:

Another thing to remember is that the doors of the spirit
world are always open between the higher minds in the
spirit world and those in the earth plane. Your spirit natures
are in constant communication with the spirit world, and if
you wish to and will listen you may receive guidance and
counsel from those Spirits who inhabit the Higher Worlds.
The spirit world is always ready and willing to give up
its secrets to you, if you are willing and ready to receive
them. "Knowledge is as free as the air you breathe, but as
air is only breathed by lungs which are ready to receive it,
and are developed up to it, so the entrance of knowledge
into a mind is determined by the capacity of that mind to
receive it. . . . Every soul gets all the knowledge to which it
is attuned. . . . There is something in Spiritualism far better
than anything you have received from it, for its capacity
and its outlook are infinite. But we must not overlook all
the seemingly little things we have learned. . . . *The fact of
communication*; that is of inestimable value."[5]

MEDIUMSHIP:

And how can we receive the truth from the higher
worlds? What are the conditions which should prevail?

In this great search for truth it is generally conceded by
those earnest workers who have worked and sought long
and patiently, that some sort of mediumship is necessary,
to investigate thoroughly, whether it be our own or that of
some one else.

---

[4] *After Death,— What*, Ernest Hunt.
[5] *The Widow's Mite*, Funk, 97.

The *spiritual séance* in which these truths are received from those Higher Ones should not be entered in a spirit of idle curiosity, or for mere selfish comfort, but there should be the desire to obtain spiritual food and knowledge, which will fit us, not only for the life to come, but for real living in this earth-life. The medium should have a deep sense of high moral and spiritual values, and the séance should be opened with aspiration and prayer. If one wishes to contact only the higher spirit friends one should strive to make spiritual progress in this life. We must also realize that upon ourselves depends the success of the venture.

The question is often asked as to why *mediums* are used as go-betweens in communicating with someone on the other side. The answer is obvious. Spirits dwell in another country from ours; if one while on earth wished to communicate with a person in a distant country, he would have to use a *medium*—although perhaps not a human one. He would use a telephone, telegraph, radio or other mechanical means of communication. The mediums in the séance room or elsewhere are therefore merely taking the place of these mechanical instruments. And in cases of materialization it is necessary that the spirit visitor use the ectoplasm of the medium in order to give it a form to make itself known to the denser physical senses of those on the physical plane, as we have explained elsewhere.

LIFE ON THE OTHER SIDE:

In reading in this volume and elsewhere about the life on the other side, the home-life, the clothes, the houses, the buildings, etc, one is amazed and astounded with the diversity of opinion,—no not of "opinion" for it is not their opinion which those who communicate with us are giving us, but rather their own individual way of *realizing* it,—diversity of *description* is better. But that is the way it should be on analysis of the observation for each one gives his report of the living as he sees it. To one, the land, the houses, the clothes, the people, the very life, is one way because that is the way he has it in his consciousness; to another it is some other way according to *his* consciousness. Both are conscientious and correct in their report. Truly, "in my Father's house are many mansions." Whatever those of the spirit world are individually conscious of, that is what exists for them.

PITFALLS:

We cannot too strongly emphasize the fact that everyone who goes through the gateway of death is not immediately transformed into an angel of beauty and goodness. Even those find their level who have been careless and indifferent about the life on the other planes, and who have committed only the *lighter* sins of self-centeredness, narrow-mindedness or indifference to their fellow-men. There are earthy spirits who find it very easy to enter the earth conditions and communicate through the mediums, and these spirits are sometimes not only frivolous and playful but are often malicious and revengeful, and do a great deal of harm if allowed to occupy the mind and attention of the sitters or medium. Surely, as we are told by St. John, we should "try the spirits, whether they are of God," (1st. John, 4, 1.) and the mediums and sitters should seek protection from such as these by asking aid from their guardian angels, by using a protecting prayer or by some other method.

The Law of Rhythm and the Karmic Law are the only controlling factors in determining the length of our stay in any one realm of the after-world, and as these two laws are founded on our own character and state of being, which we give ourselves by our thoughts, words, and actions on the earth plane, the duration of our stay is still subject to our free will.

Phenomenal Spiritualism is not for all. Many minds are not able to reconcile the *phenomena* with the *greatness of the truth* of Spiritualism. Such as these must be content with the knowledge gained from the study of the principles and from the experiences of others. To them will be given the full and glorious realization that all they have actually learned on this earth-plane is true, only when they pass over to the spirit-world.

"In earth-life I did my best to help and enlighten. . . . Since my arrival in this land I have tried to carry on and to greatly increase the amount and sphere of this same work. I must impress upon you all,—the interested and the disinterested, the believer in this great subject called 'Spiritualism,' and the skeptic,—to remember that you are still on Earth, and you still have to perform the duties of Earth. You have your daily lives to lead, and you must always do well the *work in hand*."[6]

It is well to keep in mind that, "spirit visitors, séance rooms, trance addresses, are of no value unless they are a doorway through which we can enter a nobler age."[7]

Either that "new world" we hear so much about is the aim and end of spiritualism, or it is no better than the old creeds it is destined to replace.

"To believe in God as the Infinite Spirit Presence of the Universe; to hold conscious communion with spirits and angels, and to live a true, noble, spiritual, Christlike life,—these constitute a Spiritualist."[8]

---

[6] *The Blue Island*, Stead, 24.
[7] *The Psychic Observer*, Oct. 25th, 1945.
[8] *Immortality*, Peebles, 98.

INDEX

The numbers below refer to chapters and not to pages

R

Rank, in other world, 8
Rays, of God, 24; names of, 4
Reality, 1
Rebirths, all around us, 3
Religion, 2
Reincarnation, purpose of, 3 Christian
  doctrine, 3
Response, to spirit visitors, 8
Responsibility, of humans to animals, 9
Rewards, not given hy God, 2

S

Samadhi, 4
School of souls, 8
Scientists, Super Cosmic, 1
Second childhood, 4
Self, Spiritual, Ray of God, 2 mentor, 2
Shells, astral, 1
Singing, reproduced by spirit visitors,
  16; in foreign tongue, 20
Slate writing, 14
Sleep, in spirit world, 24
Soul immortal, 1
Soulless animal, 2
Souls, none lost, 4
Spirit, active principle; 1
Spirit life degree of, 24
Spirits, mischievous, 8
Spiritualism, universal panacea 24; its
  message, 1; phenomenal 24; what
  is it, 1
Spiritualist service of, 24; what is a, 24

Spirituality, in Higher Realms 25; must
  be sought, 2
State craft, aim of, 1
Suicide; 4; war case of, 23

T

Teachers, 1
Telepathy, 20
Terhune, Albert Payson, 9
Though forms, 1
Times, signs of the, 6
Title, over there, 8
Trance, astral, 4
Transition, no death, 5
Transports, 22
Truths, 1, 24

U

Ultimates, seven, 1
Unfoldment, law of, 1
Unity, of all things, 1
Universe why, 1

V

Vibration, 1
Voice box, 16

W

Wealth, only true, 24
Web, protective, 4
Weights, of mediums, 15
World, of things, origin of, 1
Worlds, of causation, 1; mental 1;
  reality of higher, 1; spiritual, 1

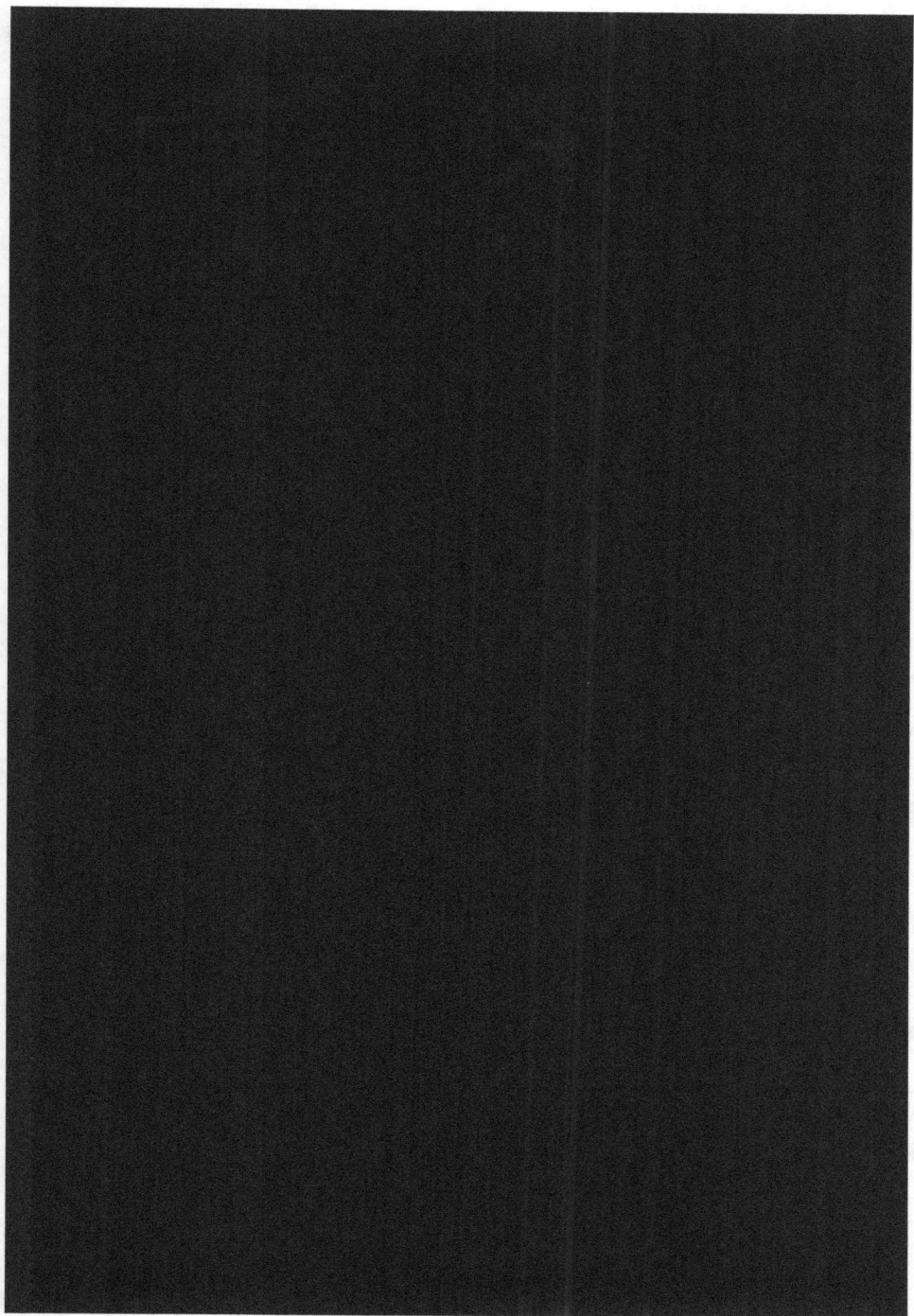

www.ingramcontent.com/pod-product-compliance
Lightning Source LLC
LaVergne TN
LVHW051623080426
835511LV00016B/2135